CW00549173

THE ANSWERS LIE WITHIN US

TO
the memory of
my parents

The Answers Lie Within Us

Towards a Science of the Human Spirit

ALISTAIR SINCLAIR
University of Glasgow

With a Foreword by
Sir Graham Hills

Ashgate

Aldershot • Brookfield USA • Singapore • Sydney

Published by
Ashgate Publishing Ltd
Gower House
Croft Road
Aldershot
Hants GU11 3HR
England

Ashgate Publishing Company
Old Post Road
Brookfield
Vermont 05036
USA

British Library Cataloguing in Publication Data
Sinclair, Alistair
    The answers lie within us : towards a science of the human
    spirit. - (Avebury series in philosophy)
    1. Life 2. Mind and body 3. Ontology 4. Life - Religious
    aspects
    I. Title
    128

Library of Congress Catalog Card Number: 98-71962

ISBN 1 84014 576 5

Printed and bound by Athenaeum Press, Ltd.,
Gateshead, Tyne & Wear.

Contents

Chapter Five - The Evaluation of Life and Living

Chapter Six - The Use and Value of the Noosphere

Chapter Seven - The Presence of Posterity

Bibliography

Name Index

Subject Index

Diagrams

Acknowledgements

I am indebted to Sir Graham Hills, former Principal of Strathclyde University, for his help and support over a lengthy gestation period during which he has been a patient midwife to the ideas in this book. Through his advice and guidance the ruggedness of earlier versions of this book has been tempered and smoothed. A much better book has ensued as a direct result of his pleas on behalf of potential readers. His suggestions for improvements to the text have been invaluable and thought-provoking.

My philosophical development was much influenced by Donald Gordon and the late Hywel Thomas both of whom supervised my M.Phil. thesis at Strathclyde University. Indeed, it was my undergraduate experience of Donald Gordon's inspired teaching of philosophy that determined me in the path of philosophy, for good or ill.

More recently, my plight as a solitary thinker has been lessened as a result of my participation as a Ph.D. student in Dr. Catherine McCall's Centre for Philosophical Inquiry at Glasgow University. Many of the ideas in this book were first exposed and subjected to rigorous criticism at philosophical inquiry sessions involving the following:

Pat Ashwell, Marilyn Bennett, Claire Cassidy, Robert Fairley, Eitan Grant, Mary Haight, Keith Hammond, Ruth Ingram, Ayisha de Lanerolle, Tony Lee, Irene Leonard, John Macintyre, Morag McClurg, Carol Peltola, Em Peterson, Andrew Pyle, Maria Figuerioa Rego, Elizabeth Roberts, Howard Robinson, Tito Tosolini, Graham Wood, and many others.

Foreword

By Sir Graham Hills

In his book, *The End of History - the Last Man,* Francis Fukuyama argued convincingly that mankind's political and ideological struggles were nearing their end. On the battlefield of history, there remained one victor, namely social democracy. This optimistic assertion was, however, subject to the caveat that three smaller dragons would still need to be slain. Those dragons were: (1) the need to ensure security and material well-being for the world's population in a sustainable environment; (2) the need to establish new identities by playing down differences in race, colour and language, and (3) the need to meet mankind's spiritual well-being whilst freeing it from religious strife.

To a good approximation, science and technology are well equipped to deal with the first. As human endeavours, they still need to learn humility and to acquire a human face but these virtues will come with humankind's greater spiritual awareness. The second requirement is a matter for education in which the new media and especially television will play a crucial part. The third, easily the most difficult, will require a better understanding of our spiritual selves and a determination to look to the future rather than to the past for the source of our moral sentiments, once solely the province of established religion.

It is at this point that this book by Alistair Sinclair steps into the picture by offering a more rational basis for human spirituality, nevertheless still rooted in the individual and that individual's psyche. Its central theme is the refinement of the human being's concept of the universe external to him or her as reflected by his or her intelligence and emotions. The collection of self-created entities which can be known and manipulated by individuals goes by the name of noosphere. This child of the human intellect is now ready to usurp the gods of the past and take over their responsibility for the well-being of humankind and especially for its posterity. This is therefore a book for both thoughtful scientists as well as thoughtful clerics.

The book has no quarrel with science. It accepts without reservation its observations and understandings. The now vast encyclopædia of articulated scientific knowledge is already a triumph of the human intellect. Its status is, of course, not omniscient. Its claims to certainty and objectivity are exaggerated and its emphasis on reductionism tiresome. But it provides a remarkably satisfactory working model of the universe and, of course, there is much more to come.

It also seems to me that this book has no quarrel with religion or religious sentiments where they do not offend scientific evidence or consistent reason. Belief is an essential precursor to any kind of thinking and it is a pre-requisite of a sustainable, civilised society to entertain a range of beliefs, for example, in the value of goodness, honesty, integrity, beauty and much else.

This book therefore recognises the historic fact that our civilised behaviour, our moral sentiments and our aesthetic values originated in religious beliefs and religious practices. To quote Lord Denning, on his retirement as Master of the Rolls.

> There can be no civilisation without the law
> There can be no law without morality, and
> There can be no morality without religion.

We should therefore regard the rise of monotheism even in its many manifestations as a vital step along the road from the jungle to civic life. But it is now time to move on.

In two matters, it is now essential to accept that, glorious though their pasts have been, all established religions carry two genetic flaws that threaten not just their existence but also that of humankind. These flaws are on the one hand spiritual and intellectual, and on the other hand painfully practical.

The spiritual flaw is the absolute refusal of almost all religions to allow for further and continued revelations of the kind that brought them into being in the first place, that is to say of the mind and will of their particular and therefore only god. They revere their pasts to the exclusion of all else. But as time passes the variety of expressions of their truths recedes further from the present and therefore from reality. Just as the word dies when it is written down so does the radiance diminish of the god of the once-and-only experience of the once-and-only prophet. A fixation with the past ensures obliviousness of the future. Damagingly it shows no consideration for posterity.

The second flaw, a corollary of the first, is the determination of religions to fight each other to the death to defend each minute idiosyncrasy distinguishing their branch of self-evidently the same religion. No cruelty has been too savage to wreak on their enemies, the infidel, the Jew, the gentile, the catholic, the protestant or simply the unbeliever.

The aim of this book is therefore to reassert the common spiritual inheritance of humankind and to give religious thought and moral sentiments a better basis on which to safeguard posterity. To do so it has had to penetrate the very essence of human awareness and human goals.

On the other hand, this book is not simply a restatement of humanism, although most humanists will resonate with its aims and its methods of argument. If anything it is the restatement, in clearer and more modern terms, of the vision and ambition of Teilhard de Chardin. His noosphere and our yearning to be at one with the world are given a better basis of belief. A new understanding of our reflective selves, and of what we can claim as our individuality, has the capacity to impart to the young a firmer sense of their purpose and their collective future which, it is hoped, will rescue them from the pain of disbelief, cynicism and aggression.

The book therefore seeks to convince thoughtful people that new thinking about religion is not only possible but essential.

PART ONE

WHAT THIS BOOK IS ABOUT

Introduction

> We are creatures of the twilight. But it is out of our race and
> lineage that minds will spring, that will reach back to us in our
> littleness to know us better than we know ourselves, and that will
> reach forward fearlessly to comprehend this future that defeats our
> eyes.   H.G. Wells, *The Discovery of the Future.*[1]

It is an interesting fact that in the English language, and perhaps no other
modern language, the future tense is represented by the verb 'to will'. An
unconscious element of human agency is thereby introduced into our
everyday use of the future tense: the future is willed just as our acts are
willed. There is the suggestion that what will be is what we will it to be,
whether we are consciously aware of this or not. This is not implied in the
dry formula: *que sera, sera*, which has a fatalistic logic about it. According
to this, people do not enter into the doing of anything in the future. In
contrast, saying 'I will do it tomorrow' invariably means 'it will be done
tomorrow'. It implies both a **prediction** of the deed to be done and an
intention to do it. The prediction stems from the intention and not *vice versa*.
Thus, in such cases the future depends on past decisions and not on a random
concurrence of events.

One is tempted to think that this feature of the English language has
contributed to the dynamism and optimism of the English-speaking peoples by
keeping their minds open to the possibility of the future being different from
the past because they will it to be so. Hence, for example, the ethos of Merrie
England in the Elizabethan and Restoration periods, the Scottish
Enlightenment, and the American Dream. However, this feature can be
traced back to Anglo-Saxon times and is found in other languages in the past,
so that a causal connection is hard to substantiate.[2]

---

[1] H.G. Wells, *The Discovery of the Future*, ed. by P. Parrinder, 1902 - London: PNL
Press, 1989, p.36. This work is further discussed and quoted in Chapter Seven, section three
of this book.
[2] According to the Oxford English Dictionary: 'The most remarkable feature of this verb,
besides its many idiomatic and phrasal uses, is its employment as a regular auxiliary of the
future tense, which goes back to the OE period, and may be paralleled in other Germanic
languages, e.g. MHG.'

This book is very much about the future and our ability to cope with it and change it according to how we visualise it should be. The 'oughtness' contained in any existing situation implies that things can be better in the future, if we so will it to be. The contents of this book comprise ways of coping with the future so that it invariably will be better if we make the effort to plan and think about it with sufficient diligence. Only the tools are offered here, for the motivation to use them must come from within each individual.

Life for everyone consists in using the lessons of the past to serve the purposes of the future. This forward-looking stance is of increasing importance now that, due to our technological prowess, the future is more under our collective control than ever. For good or evil, the human race has assumed responsibility for moulding the future in its own image, simply because of its increasing technological capabilities. This presents humankind with awesome opportunities as well as potentials for catastrophe.

To make the best of these opportunities and to avoid the potential catastrophes, it is necessary to develop and strengthen the human spirit. People's confidence and self-reliance must be boosted but only in so far as they retain a realistic attitude towards what they can and should do in the world to make things better and not worse. This is the main purpose in developing an independent science of the human spirit; a science which is not dependent on the materialism of the empirical sciences on the one hand or hamstrung by religious sentiment and dogma on the other hand. The views of science and religion tend towards opposite extremes: the former view towards materialism, reductionism and mechanism; the latter view towards spiritualism, superstition and mysticism. Human beings, as ever, lie somewhere in the middle ground which remains to be made sense of.

An attempt is made in this book to make sense of the conflicts and differences between the scientific and religious views. While science apparently stands triumphant over what remains of religion, the latter has nevertheless survived this onslaught. Religion is not likely to lie down and die while it has much of value to offer us which scientific knowledge has not yet taken account of. But what is worth preserving about religion needs to be distinguished from what is not worth preserving. For instance, there seems to be general agreement that authoritarianism, dogmatism, bigotry, narrow-mindedness and other disapproved-of consequences of religious activity are to be discarded.

It is argued here that if religion can be purged of whatever tends towards its negative and inhuman consequences, such as sectarian divisions and enforced orthodoxy, then it will become compatible with the scientific view and take its place among the sciences in representing the spiritual aspect of human beings. In this way, it will be able to temper the excesses to which the scientific view leads, without threatening to bring all scientific endeavour to an end, as religion has done all too often in the past. The result is not a new form of religion in the old sense but a new form of science which takes account of the religious experience of humankind. It will not have those undesirable consequences because it will be scientific, self-critical, and ultimately refutable and replaceable in its detailed development.

This book pinpoints those aspects of religion that are perennial and part of the human condition. It incorporates those aspects in a science of human spirit which might replace religion in its generally accepted form. The implications of this view have apparently never been worked out in any great detail. The task of doing so is begun in this book.

It is argued here that religion in its usual form has had its day and it is time to move on to something better and more in keeping with the times we live in. For instance, most people wish to enjoy the benefits of modern civilisation **now** and to make the most of their lives **now** and not wait for allegedly better things in the hereafter. The notion of a heaven or paradise belongs to a bygone age when life was full of misery and disease, from birth till death. The view offered by the science of the human spirit outlined here places a high value on the healthy-minded enjoyment of life in the here-and-now.

This book will therefore be of interest to those who question the value of religion as it stands and see the need to replace those aspects of it which are no longer appropriate to the times we now live in. It may also help those who are looking for answers beyond the usual religious ones. It offers a new science of the human spirit which is not itself the answer but which may help people to find answers to such questions as 'Why am I here?', 'What is the point of my existence?' and 'What is the value of life?'

In dealing with the ends of life and living, this book shares the humanist aim of pursuing these ends without resorting to outmoded or supernatural beliefs. It offers a number of ways of evaluating the purpose of life and of the living of it from day to day. It does so by putting the human spirit, as defined herein, at the fountain-head of all value, meaning and purpose in the universe. In starker terms, the activity of the human spirit is held responsible for attributing whatever meaning or value that material objects are worthy of acquiring. There is no more reason or purpose in the universe than we, as intelligent beings, put into it. But we are not responsible for the existence of external things, nor for the measure of them, only for the **act** of measuring them. The world is independent of our perceiving or conceiving it. Nevertheless, it is subject to our acts of perceiving or conceiving it, and may be purposely changed for better or worse as a result of what we do. What we need to be clear about, as an intelligent species, are the best possible reasons for changing the world. This science examines the means of arriving at such reasons, and this forms the moral basis of the science of the human spirit.

This is a large undertaking of which this short book is only a preliminary study or sketch. Much remains to be done in developing this new and radical viewpoint. Its continued development depends on how well it is received by those interested in its aims. But hopefully, enough has been done to make clear what is being attempted, however deficient this interim analysis is conceived to be.

The basic arguments of the second part of this book may be summarised as follows:

    ♦ The human spirit is a goal-seeking mental activity which is brain-centred and has no transcendental origin. That activity is spiritual in that it is self-referential, that is to say, turned in upon itself to create self-identity. In so far as goals are sought in relation to the self, then they reflect the spirit of the individual. This aspect of mental activity is essentially non-material but is nevertheless firmly rooted in the physical activity of the brain and the central nervous system.

    ♦ In fulfilling our goals in a purposeful way, we confer value and meaning on things which otherwise lack all value and meaning. Being a spiritual entity therefore consists in actively pursuing ends, aims, and goals which introduce value and meaning into a universe fundamentally devoid of these without such activity.

    ♦ What is important about our spiritual activity is the way that we confer value and meaning on things in a **holistic** manner. That is to say, we grasp things as a whole in pursuing our ends and goals. This ability to grasp things as a whole enables us to act effectively in a universe which is otherwise potentially chaotic and unfathomable.

    ♦ We confer value and meaning on the material universe by our use of universal notions such as the universe, life, good, and beauty, which are not things or 'mental furniture' but the means of relating ourselves to the universe and its contents while differentiating ourselves at the same time. They are 'work-in-process' and lack fixed meanings or definitions because they are interacting processes rather than stable mental objects.

♦ Such universal notions act as **evaluators** performing an ethical function which does not involve the imposition of moral codes. They allow people to perform their own evaluations of their aims and purposes, if they so wish. Thus, the good for everyone is not considered here, only the good which people discover for themselves and within themselves. In that sense, Adam Smith's 'invisible hand' is extended from economic to moral matters.

♦ What unifies us in spite of our individuality, is our pursuit of common goals in realising our own needs, desires, and inclinations. We are able to come together in large and small groups because of the means of communication which we have in common as language-using intelligent beings. This unifying and grouping together in pursuit of common goals takes place within the noosphere of communicable thought. The noosphere is a name for the activity of everyone communicating with each other throughout the globe. It provides the rationale for a pluralistic, democratic society and unifies all our differences while tolerating them. For it has no more control over us than the Internet (which is a part of the noosphere). Nevertheless, this notion can be used by us to regulate our behaviour in relation to others, in our own self-interest. Thus, the overall evaluator of our social values and meanings is the noosphere within which all our agreements and disagreements are sorted out, or not, as the case may be. It is not that the noosphere does anything to us in evaluating our behaviour; it is merely that we ourselves of our own freewill accept the arbitration of the noosphere in merely being moral agents.

♦ Even so, the noosphere is only the **immediate** arbiter of values and meanings. The **ultimate** arbiter is posterity, that is to say, the future generations of human beings, or failing these, intelligent beings in general. For if the human race should not survive in its present form, we can be reasonably confident that intelligent beings in some form will exist in the future, through evolution, colonisation or whatever. Thus, in confronting problems and difficulties, we can strive to imagine and estimate how these may appear to posterity to avoid current prejudices and present limitations of thought.

♦ Scientific and other types of knowledge comprise a significant **part** of the noosphere, and our acceptable contributions to such knowledge are worthy offerings to posterity. Developing and improving our factual and theoretical knowledge is a task vital to the future not only of our species or of any intelligent species but also of life on this or any other planet. Such knowledge, and particularly scientific knowledge, can be a bulwark against the vagaries of chance and misfortune to which uninformed nature is subject. It is also invaluable to us in the present for ascertaining and assessing our place in the universe. The data of science are to be acquired not just for their own sake but also because they enable us to evaluate our lives relative to the universe as a whole. Thus, our witnessing, as individuals, the scientists' growing understanding of the universe and its contents adds to the interest and significance of our everyday lives. Such discoveries also increase the value of life in general.

This system of thought is a viable substitute for religion only in so far as it deals with our spiritual nature and provides a means of accounting for our place in the universe. Whether it is any more successful in assuming the role which religion currently plays in society than past attempts such as Marxism and positivism, remains to be seen. Certainly, there is no question of advocating the abolition or suppression of religion institutions. At most, they will wither away in the face of a more attractive and satisfying substitute, of which this study only provides a theoretical structure. The institutional structure of any viable alternative to organised religion is not given here, since the purpose of this study is to open up the debate about this, in the expectation that an appropriate alternative will be forthcoming.

This system of thought may appear not to be sufficient in itself to replace organised religion because it differs from religion in regarding nothing as so sacred, supernatural, or superhuman that it may not be dealt with rationally and sensibly. This seemingly precludes the emotional and unfathomable aspects of religion where these are incompatible with rational thought. But there is much that scientific knowledge cannot and does not attempt to explain. This science of the human spirit enters into the mystical and mysterious aspects of the human condition, life and the universe but only in the scientific spirit of attempting to make sense of them. Unlike the physical sciences, it entertains those aspects because they are mysterious and mystical, though it does not attempt to explain everything about them. It nevertheless provides a framework within which these aspects may be discussed and acted upon rather than being considered beyond our ken altogether, as is the case with traditional religion. Thus, the ultimate connection between ourselves and the universe is treated here as an unfathomable mystery, an understanding of which we can only approach by slow degrees. But we cannot even begin to make sense of this mystery if we put everything into the hands of a God to whose level of intelligence we can never aspire.

Though an attempt is here being made to rethink religion, this is not a matter of reconciling religion with science. So-called reconciliations seem only to head in either of two directions: either towards reducing the claims of the Bible to those of 'presenting in its substance the truth about God and our relation to him'[3]; or towards supplying a religion of science or humanity which, as in the case of religious cults such as the Unification Church and Scientology, do little for either science or humanity but a lot for the egos of those enforcing their views on others. In contrast, the approach here is to replace the viewpoint of past religions and to account for the religious dimension in human thought by using entirely different terms, e.g. the noosphere and posterity

The importance of such notions as noosphere and posterity lies in their countering accusations of relativism and amorality which are directed at those who deny the existence of any God or supernatural being. It is thought by some that, without an absolute being, there can be no absolute values in which case all behaviour is relative and equally permissible.[4] In simple terms, you can do what you like because there is no Big Daddy out there to tell you otherwise. However, it is argued in this book that both the noosphere and posterity provide standpoints or Archimedean leverage points[5] from which we can evaluate our own behaviour without resort to external compulsion. This is argued in Parts Five and Six.

The term 'religion' here refers to those supernatural beliefs, rituals and writings which are not based on material evidence but which are to be accepted on faith and unquestionable authority. It signifies an adherence to beliefs, rituals, and writings which is uncritical and is based on their unquestioned authority. So far from being a religion in that sense, the new

---

[3]   H.D. Lewis, *Philosophy of Religion*, (London: English Universities Press, 1965), p.58.

[4]   Cf. the remarks of F.C. Copleston in conversation with Bertrand Russell in *The Existence of God*, (ed. John Hick - London: Macmillan, 1964), pp.168 & 185f. Russell thought that our intuitive recognition of good and bad is sufficient to keep us on the straight and narrow.

[5]   Cf. Bernard Williams, *Ethics and the Limits of Philosophy*, (London: Fontana, 1987), ch. 2, p.22f.

science of the human spirit described here is based on the evidence of our experiences, both internal and external, and on the evidence of human culture and science. Such evidence is used to evaluate the impact of our spiritual activity in giving significance to life, society, and the universe at large. This spiritual activity is moreover internal to us and part of what we normally do in our everyday lives. This is discussed further in Chapter Three.

The term 'science' here includes all those disciplines that rely on evidence, observation, investigation, and experiment to examine the nature of reality. A science owes nothing to pre-conceived theories concerning what might be the case. It is concerned to establish what is really the case in fundamental terms. Thus, the science of the human spirit is scientific in so far as it examines how we actually confer value and meaning on things, and it attempts to account for such matters in a systematic and conclusive manner.

It may appear that in laying down a scientific basis for our spirituality, the emotional side of our nature is being downgraded in some way. On the contrary, the irrational emotionalism of fundamentalist religion are to be replaced by the 'rational passions'[6] that underlie our intellectual endeavours:

> A love of truth and a contempt for lying, a concern for accuracy in observation and inference, and a corresponding repugnance of error in logic or fact. It demands revulsion at distortion, disgust at evasion, admiration of theoretical achievement, respect for the considered argument of others.
> A passionate drive for *clarity*, accuracy, and fair-mindedness, a fervor for getting to the bottom of things . . . for listening sympathetically to opposition points of view, a compelling drive to seek out evidence, an intense aversion to contradiction, sloppy thinking, inconsistent application of standards, a devotion to truth as against self-interest - [which are] essential components of the rational person.[7]

These are the passions that characterise the society we live in and the ones which do credit to our civilisation. They encourage openmindedness, curiosity and an abhorrence of complacency and selfishness. They lead on to better things whereas the emotionalism of fundamentalist religion tend to bring reason and thought to an end. This point is developed further in Chapter Two of this book.

---

6   Cf. Harvey Siegel, *Educating Reason*, (New York: Routledge, 1988), p.40.
7   *Ibid.* As quoted by Siegel from two different authors, I. Scheffler and R.S. Peters, respectively.

At the same time, an equal and opposite emphasis on the value of our religious experiences does not mean, for instance, that a religion of humanity is here being advocated; least of all, in the manner of Auguste Comte (1798-1857), whose Church of Humanity[8] complete with priests, prayers, hymns and rituals, was Roman Catholicism by another name. For instance, his approach was to take an arbitrary list of famous people, make saints of them, and assign dates on the calendar for each one. Even so, Comte's positivism anticipated some of the views expressed here. In particular, he used the term 'humanity' in much the same way as the term 'noosphere' is used here. But to worship 'Humanity' as if it were a god or 'supreme being' is clearly going to the same extremes as religion at its most dogmatic.

In this book, the idea of a revealed, dogmatic religion is replaced by a notion of spirituality in terms of the value and significance which we bring into our lives and the lives of others by means of our own spiritual activity. According to this view, nothing inhuman is worthy of being worshipped, idolised, or otherwise put on a pedestal. Neither the noosphere nor posterity, for instance, are to be deified or sanctified. They are to be worked for in fulfilling our best and highest purposes as human beings. The achievements of the human race are certainly worthy of admiration but the effect of worshipping them is to exalt the past rather than to contribute to future well-being. Such an exaltation of the past is a feature of present-day organised religion which prevents it from contributing meaningfully to posterity and hence threatens its own future.

This book offers a consistent system of thought about such matters of religion, and in being a system it purports to contribute to scientific thought. Whether it succeeds in that regard depends on its acceptance by the community of like-minded thinkers who use its conclusions to find answers to the fundamental questions being considered here. For this endeavour to be scientific, it must also be possible for these sympathetic thinkers to find fault with the detail of its arguments and conclusions, and thus to improve on them and develop them. Plainly this book contains only the rudiments and foundations of this science and not the final truth of the matter.

---

[8] Comte's absurd form of religion was taken up by some eccentrics in Victorian England where four temples of humanity - two in London, one each in Liverpool and Newcastle - were established. The Liverpool temple lingered on till 1947 when it was sold and became the Third Church of Christ Scientist. Its statue of humanity (a mother with child) appropriately 'gathered dust in Liverpool Maternity Hospital'. (Cf. Terence R. Wright, *The Religion of Humanity: The Impact of Comtean Positivism on Victorian Britain*, [Cambridge: CUP, 1986], p.260.)

The arguments of this book are also a contribution to humanist thought in that they start from the human being and extend outwards to the universe at large. The suggestion that in doing so we are guilty of 'arrogance' in placing ourselves at the centre of things is strongly repudiated here as being unworthy of us. Such an accusation is justified only if we were to build on our human experience in an uncritical way and without recognition of the severe limitations to our powers and abilities in achieving anything of lasting significance on this planet. Knowing what we can or cannot do and what we should or should not do, must be the basis for all our actions, especially those that might have long term consequences on the biosphere and the material resources of the planet. The noosphere can no more exist without the biosphere than the mind can without the brain. We are only arrogant in so far as we are thoughtless and unmindful of these consequences. Indeed, we may expose our limitations in that direction by clarifying our place in the universe.

The importance of knowing what we can or cannot do without harming our environment means that scientific research is indispensible to our future. For that reason, this book supports scientists in their endeavour to understand our environment and the universe in which we live. Its possible contribution to the future of this scientific endeavour is that of clarifying the role of science in human affairs. It is a happy thought that we acquire scientific knowledge quite naturally in fulfilling our collective goals at the same time as we indulge our child-like sense of wonder at the amazing world in which we live.[9]

The answers mentioned in the title of this book are only the subjective answers concerning our goals and aims. Objective answers concerning the physical world are not being referred to. Furthermore, what is offered in this book are not the answers themselves but the way to find our own answers to fundamental questions by reaching inside ourselves to explore the notions of value and meaning, and such universal notions as the universe, life, good and beauty.

If there is a single message it is that we are here to fulfil purposes which each one of us must seek within ourselves and not elsewhere. This great task assumes that we are equipped with the tools for conducting such a search **not** because we were necessarily born with them but simply because we are an intelligent species living in a co-operative society. For the purposeful application of the spirit within us requires not only inner willingness but also social conditions which bring out the best in us without being repressive or intolerant.

[9]   Though this view is not shared by scientists such as Lewis Wolpert in his book, *The Unnatural Nature of Science*, London: Faber and Faber, 1993.

1 Finding the Answers for Ourselves

> The true physics is that which will, one day, achieve the inclusion of man in his wholeness in a coherent picture of the world.
>
> Pierre Teilhard de Chardin[1]

1 The Need for Spirituality in Our Lives

It is a commonplace to say that we live in an increasingly materialistic society but it is not always made clear what this means. It does not just mean that people are obsessed with possessing more and more material goods. Their materialist bias also consists in a mindless commitment to the rat race. It means increasingly selling their souls to their jobs, careers, pop idols, or hobbies to the exclusion of the wider perspective. In so far as they narrow their interests and pre-occupations to progressively fewer things, they lose touch with the wider unifying theme to which everything belongs. It is argued here that this unifying theme is not God or anything supernatural but is that which results from our sharing what we all have in common as human beings, that is to say, the human spirit within us.

In narrowing people's interests and pre-occupations, this growing materialism shortens time scales and discourages individuals from delaying their choices. What seems to be important and valuable at the present moment must be sought, bought, experienced, or fulfilled without further thought or delay. In this seeking of instant gratification, people lose control over their needs and desires, ultimately becoming enslaved by them. They make more and more out of less and less, and in so doing forfeit their freedom to be themselves. In crowding their lives with trivia, they lose sight of the things that are of real and lasting importance in life. These things are as much spiritual as material, since they concern the value and importance of human relationships, as well as the universe as a whole. Our lives, and the quality we bring into them, are of greater importance than the material surroundings in which we live them. Unless we know the value that we put on material objects

---

[1] *The Phenomenon of Man*. London: Collins, 1959, p.40.

13

and know what we want to do with them, there seems little point in having them. Such knowledge is basically a spiritual matter in that it has no material existence outside our thinking about it.

This book aims to help people wean themselves from their bias towards materialism, as this bias results from the failure of religious teaching to restore the balance between the material and spiritual viewpoints. It is argued here that the strength and comfort of our spiritual well-being can no longer be found in dogmatic beliefs but in the process of looking into ourselves and evaluating our inner life. We begin exploring the human spirit when we attempt to make sense of the values that we attach to our subjective feelings and experiences. This is a first step towards satisfying ourselves about the ultimate value of our lives, as will be made clearer in the rest of this book.

However, in stressing the importance of our spiritual side, the value of the material world is not thereby rejected. Material comfort and security is required to ensure that our spiritual values can flourish and develop. A bed of nails or fanatical asceticism will do little or nothing for our spiritual creativity. Yet many religions have advocated and still advocate penances, fasts, flagellation, and other forms of self-punishment as the way to faith and to set oneself right with God. Thus, we must guard against going from one extreme of material comfort to another extreme of spiritual mortification. The view of the human spirit being developed here eschews such extremes because our spirit is here seen as an activity directed towards ends, rather than as an end in itself wasted in mindless meditation and endless contemplation.

These considerations involve one of the principal questions being addressed in this work, namely, 'What could replace existing religion without itself being a religion?' What is proposed in place of religion is a science of the human spirit which covers the area of theology without referring to the existence of any ultimate being such as a god. Since we can have no knowledge of ultimate or final causes, what is refuted in this work is not the existence of any god but the value of the notion of god. For it does not really matter whether anything called god really exists or not. What matters are the undesirable consequences of continuing to use this notion, namely, the enmity and divisions that result from the impossibility of arriving at any generally acceptable notion of what this god is or is not. Also, there is the question of the extent to which belief in an unknown and unknowable god impedes the search for our spiritual selves, in other words, our soul. In other words, the very idea of god may in fact do us more harm than good.

2 Finding out for Ourselves Why We Are Here

> A Christian says: 'If all were good, all would be happy'. A socialist
> says: 'If all were happy, all would be good'. A fascist says: 'If all
> obeyed the state, all would be both happy and good'. A lama says: 'If
> all were like me, happiness and goodness would not matter'. A
> humanist says: 'Happiness and goodness need more analysis'. This
> last is the least deniable view.   John Fowles.[2]

'What's it all about?' is another question dealt with here. Basically, the reason why we are here is to find out why we are here, both as individuals and as an intelligent species. Science has already gone some way towards giving us the answers in terms of the physical composition of the universe. But to tackle the difficult question of what we are meant to do in this material universe, we must find the answers within ourselves. It is the contention of this book that there is no god out there waiting to help us, and the past history of religion, as a perpetual source of conflict, cruelty, and inhumanity, is evidence that it is not helpful for us to believe that there might be. People continue to fight and kill each other in the name of such a being. They do so because it is anybody's guess what their god is really like and whose side it is or is not supporting. There can never be any agreement over the matter.

The precise information that science now gives us about the universe and its contents, should enable the human race to be strong and confident enough to stand on its own feet and to determine its own future. But religion undermines this strength and confidence because it belongs to the adolescence of the human race when people were so ignorant and fearfully dependent on superstition that they required a mythical, father figure or earth mother to cling to. The difference which scientific knowledge has made, lies in the realisation that we may now rely on science to tackle most diseases and disasters and that we need no longer meekly submit to the will of God as if nothing more can be done.

By definition, the religious standpoint subordinates us forever to an infinitely more perfect and superior being than ourselves. This stunts our desire to better ourselves and take care of ourselves and the world around us. In stressing the weaknesses of human nature, it overlooks the strengths we derive from our collective endeavours. This is especially so when these are conducted for the best of motives, not least in setting right the excesses and

---

[2] John Fowles, *The Aristos*, London: Triad/Granada, 1980, p.110.

mistakes of past human endeavours, environmental or otherwise, none of which are palliated by prevailing religious beliefs.

Sadly, most religions are inevitably backward-looking often to the point of ancestor worship or of deifying long dead corpses. Instead it is to posterity that we must look as being our ultimate goal and our greatest responsibility. We may not arrive at all the answers concerning why we are here, but our successors may do so, provided we ensure that there is a future for them. We must look to this future to solve the more intractable of our problems. Therefore, everything must be done in the present to ensure there is a rich and productive posterity for us.

It is to be hoped that this work will open up a new field of study concerned to establish why we are here. This can only be done in the light of current scientific knowledge and not in accordance with religious views formulated to meet people's needs hundreds or thousands of years ago. In time, the science of the human spirit may well replace religion as a concept. In practice that is not its aim since, unlike religion itself, it does not seek to alter people's personal beliefs. It aims only to provide individuals with the means of establishing their own personal beliefs.

3 The Need for a Science of the Human Spirit

> Of myself I say nothing; but in behalf of the business which is in hand I entreat men to believe that it is not an opinion to be held, but a work to be done; and to be well assured that I am labouring to lay the foundation, not of a sect or doctrine, but of human utility and power.
> Francis Bacon.[3]

In so far as religion is of little relevance to the complicated world we live in, there is a need for a science of the human spirit to account for the spiritual aspect of human nature without resorting to theological imponderables. This science of the human spirit concerns the relationship of human beings to themselves and to the universe of which they form an inextricable part. It is argued here that this relationship, as revealed by science, is mysterious

---

[3]   Preface to 'The Great Instauration' in *The Philosophical Works of Francis Bacon*, (London: 1905), p.247. This is part of the Latin quotation which Kant added to the beginning of his second edition of *The Critique of Pure Reason*. The quotation also appears at the beginning of J.G. Fichte's first introduction to his *Wissenschaftlehre*, (trans. by P. Heath & J. Lachs as *The Science of Knowledge*, [Cambridge: CUP 1982], p.3).

enough without postulating the existence of gods, angels, aliens, demons, devils, and the like.

Even though there is no god worth speaking of, we have still to justify the place of humankind in the universe and the role which the human spirit plays in it. We can show that the workings of the universe produce intelligent beings quite naturally, without any design or purpose, and that it is up to us to make what we can of our place in the universe.

There is a need for a science of the human spirit which views the universe from within ourselves rather than from the point of view of physical reality. The physical sciences examine the universe objectively and reduce its workings to fundamental principles. But the science of the human spirit takes a holistic view of the universe rather than a reductive one. It examines the way the human mind views the universe in terms of wholes and goals.

The name tentatively used here for this science is **noology**. This word is much older than the word 'noosphere' as it was first used by several 17th century German writers (Colovius, Mejerus, Wagnerus, Zeidlerus) but more notably by Kant as 'the rationalistic theory of innate ideas'. But it is the use of the term by the German philosopher, Rudolf C. Eucken (1846-1926), which is the clinching factor:

> Eucken distinguished noological method from the psychological
> and cosmological. Its object is the Spiritual Life, *i.e.* the source of
> Reality, and the self-contained goal in which man participates.[4]

The principal purpose of this work is to establish the basis of this science of noology. It seeks to re-interpret our spiritual capacities from a scientific rather than a religious point of view. Though it deals with the spiritual realm which is traditionally the sphere of religion, it is not a religion since it demands no unreasoned belief or faith. It dispassionately considers the spiritual aspect of our human experience as distinct from the material aspects dealt with by the physical sciences. It is a science of the adventure of the human spirit and hence of our goal-oriented nature. It draws attention to the intimate connection between our striving for goals and the spiritual unity within us which makes such striving possible. Understanding the nature of the

---

[4] *Dictionary of Philosophy*, ed. by D.D. Runes, New Jersey: Littlefield, Adams, 1977. p.212. However, Eucken was not a systematic thinker and was not even well-regarded by British Idealists such as Bradley and Bosanquet. Cf. J. Passmore, *A Hundred Years of Philosophy*, London: Penguin, 1968, p.85.

spirit within us is the key to understanding what we are in relation to the universe as a whole. To that extent, the answer to it all yet lies within us.

Noology attempts to justify the scientific view of the universe as against those aspects of religion which are incompatible with and antithetical to science. Unlike the religious view, noology does not oppose the physical sciences but endorses and makes use of them. It takes its place alongside the other sciences in its accounting for the presence of the human spirit in the material universe as described by science. For it is argued here that the human spirit requires science for its enlargement and development as much as science requires the human spirit for its continued progress. Without science, we cannot formulate precise and reliable goals for ourselves. Without the human spirit, science fulfils no purpose outside itself.

Noology is concerned with identifying the value added to the universe by the goal-fulfilling behaviour of living beings and ourselves in particular. It examines how the human spirit differentiates itself from physical reality by conceptualising the contents of that reality. Our acts of apprehending and conceptualising reality put value and meaning into the objects of apprehension and conceptualisation, without which they are nothing but material objects.

In a sense, the universe is nothing without us. However, in another sense, it is everything without us: in evaluative terms it is the former; in realistic terms the latter. Thus, 'man is the measure of all things' applies only where measurement means subjective evaluation, and not physical measurement. With the latter, we measure what is already there; with the former we introduce our own values by which the universe acquires meaning and purpose it lacked without them. The given universe is there to be measured and evaluated but gains by these acts a spiritual significance which transcends the undifferentiated matter of which it is ultimately composed.

At the same time, noology does not deify the universe. It treats it as an organism of which we form a part and with which we live in harmony by our acquiescence in what is physically necessary. It is no god as it is far from perfect, being no better than us, possibly worse. Also, it does nothing for us except give us the opportunity of living and of making use of its energy and matter for our own purposes.

This new science differs from psychology in that it deals with the objects of mental activity rather than the physical and observable nature of that activity. It is concerned not with the physical and behavioural events involved in intending anything, but with what that intention is directed towards as an end and why it is so intended. Also, psychology is concerned with past and present events, whereas the science of the human spirit is directed towards future events. This is so because it is concerned with ends and purposes which can only look ahead and anticipate the future.

Noology is a kind of bridge between psychology and biology. It resembles the latter in so far as it deals with the goal-oriented aspect of human beings but it does so from the viewpoint of what is being done in the mind. Both these sciences examine the human being objectively, but it is left to the science of the human spirit to deal with the subjectivity of human thought and action which makes goals and ends out of the intentional objects of mental activity.

4 Some Further Implications of Noology

Noology also implies contentions such as the following, not all of which are discussed comprehensively in this book:

> That the ends of human race are the chief concern of a science of the human spirit; such ends as why the human race is here and what it is to do with itself in the universe. It is not concerned with the biological or organic functioning of human beings. Nor it does not describe human beings from a material or physical point of view. As is argued in Chapter Three, this science is about the dualism that seems to be inherent in organic beings: a dualism in the form of an interaction between their unified internal workings and the context in which these works take place. This interaction is important in ensuring that the organism has ends that are distinct from anything else existing in the physical world.

> That, on the whole, the ends of the individual serve the ends of the human race, even though the individual may not have the latter ends in mind when formulating his own (thus applying Smith's 'invisible hand' to noospheric matters as well as economic ones). This does not mean overestimating the importance of the human race in the scheme of things. It means only ascertaining its proper place in the universe by showing how its ends are dependent on the ends of the individual and not vice versa (which is what happens when the ends of religion override those of the individual).

> That the expression of morality lies not in adopting a moralistic or authoritarian stance but by showing how the good of the human race flows naturally from each person pursuing their own good in

their own way. This does not mean emphasising the freedom of the individual or an 'anything goes' attitude. On the contrary, it makes people responsible for pursuing their own ends rationally and sensibly so that their freedom is dependent on their taking on that responsibility and is not inalienable or sacrosanct. In other words, everyone is responsible to everyone else to show that they are worthy of the freedoms bestowed on them. But the responsibility remains with the individual and not with external authority or any social organisation. Lack of responsibility on the part of the individual has to be shown and not just immorality, illegality or criminality. The last named are symptomatic of that lack and are not ends in themselves. If they were really ends in themselves then there would no exception to the strict and absolute imposition of rules, laws or moral codes, no matter what the individual's real intentions and motivations were.

➤ That the process of formulating ends is a holistic one that involves the use of inductive as opposed to deductive reasoning. To find his true ends, the individual must look at life as a whole so as to take into account as many facts and factors as possible and to overlook as little as possible. Failure to do so, narrows the conclusions arrived at and renders them less realistic and practical. Furthermore, it is argued that this ability to comprehend wholes as being more than the sum of their parts comes from a turning in of human thought into itself. This turning in, or **palintropy**, is the mechanism by which inductive reasoning generalises and abstracts from a mass of particulars. And it is the mechanism by which we establish our identity as unique persons in the universe (and not just as members of human society).

➤ That the effect of formulating ends is to look to the future with the aim of changing it for better or for worse. We usually look to the future by imagining it in terms of what we value and judge to have better or worse consequences for ourselves or others. We do so by applying such universal notions as good, truth, beauty, justice etc. This activity is here called 'noology'.

➤ That the fulfilment of the legitimate ends of the human race implies its advancement. This means working out what these ends are in the context of the contemporary society in which we live. Each generation has the responsibility re-thinking these ends in light of the good or ill achieved by past generations.

➤ That the end of all human advancement is to develop the noosphere of communicable thought and action. For it is through the development of the noosphere that the individual is offered greater opportunities of self-expression and material and spiritual enrichment. Its nature is such that its growth consists in more thoughtfulness and purposefulness being introduced into human activity than previously. This increased diversity provides more opportunity for people to make something of themselves and their lives. And the same increase in diversity can also contribute to economic growth and development so that there is no question of material prosperity being lessened as a result of implying this science of the human spirit.

2 Rethinking Religion and Morality

> We have known people who, having the appearance of great zeal in religion, have yet wanted even the common affections of humanity, and shown themselves extremely degenerate and corrupt. Others again, who have paid little regard to religion, and been considered as mere atheists, have yet been observed to practise the rules of morality, and act in many cases with such good meaning and affection towards mankind as might seem to force an acknowledgement of their being virtuous.
>
> Earl of Shaftesbury (1711)[1]

> The objections to religion are of two sorts - intellectual and moral. The intellectual objection is that there is no reason to suppose any religion true; the moral objection is that religious precepts date from a time when men were more cruel than they are, and therefore tend to perpetuate inhumanities which the moral conscience of the age would otherwise outgrow.
>
> Bertrand Russell (1930)[2]

1 The Irrelevance of Religion Today

Religion needs to be rethought to provide those for whom religion already means little or nothing with something worth believing in. It is unavoidable that unacceptable aspects of organised religion come under attack in the process. Particularly objectionable is the kind of religion which imposes its views on people by authoritarian means because it assumed to comprehend the whole truth about the human condition. Such religious imposition belittles people in the name of some allegedly superior being whom no one really knows anything about, as is argued in section two below.

---

[1] Anthony Ashley Cooper, 3rd Earl of Shaftesbury, *Characteristics of Men, Manners, Opinions, Times,* 1711 - ed. J.M. Robertson - New York: Bobbs-Merrill, 1964, p.237.

[2] Bertrand Russell, 'Has Religion Made Useful Contributions to Civilisation?' *Why I am not a Christian,* London: Unwin, 1975, p.31.

Religion of the authoritarian sort being condemned here does not include, for instance, what William James called 'the religion of healthy mindedness'[3] where it consists in having a positive, cheerful, and optimistic attitude of mind and not in adopting a systematic religious view of any kind. Being enthusiastic about life and its possibilities is not a religion but a philosophy or way of living. In contrast, the saintly, self-immolating way of life is usually the product of religion, often of the worst, most negative sort. Thus, a healthy-minded approach to life is our natural state of mind and does not necessarily require a religion to instil it. But a restrictive, negative approach to life usually does require religion which provides the rationale and motivations for adopting the resultant discomfort and distress. While going to extremes of behaviour is usually bad for us, it is clear from James's work that religion fosters such extremes as much as it moderates them.

If people want to be unhappy, tested, challenged, and stretched in mind and body, they should do so for the best possible reasons. But the religious mentality makes such tests and challenges into ends in themselves. This means there is no end to them except to become a ragged, demented hermit living in a desert, like the anchorites of Egypt in the fourth century AD. And there is no end to them because such individuals believe that they are perfecting themselves in pursuit of godliness. But they are living to no human or rational purpose at all since no human being is capable of approaching the perfection of God, even if it were known for certain what that perfection consisted in.

Religion in the usual sense of the word is therefore not the way forward for humankind. None of the religions available, either in the past or the present, have ever reached any agreement amongst themselves about their beliefs, even when they have a common origin, as in the case of Christianity and Judaism. In fact, it appears that the more that religions have in common, the more emnity, aggression, and mistrust there is between them because they need to differentiate themselves from each other, as in the case of Protestants and Catholics in Northern Ireland, or the Roman Catholic, Greek Orthodox, and Islamic faiths among the Serbo-Croat peoples.

It has to be said that all the traditional religions, Judaism, Islam, Buddhism, and Hinduism, as well as Christianity, are relics of the past that have had their day. They are all interesting from a scholarly point of view, and they have much to teach us from practical and personal points of view. The Bible and other religious scriptures are great works of literature to be

---

[3] William James, *Varieties of Religious Experience*, 1902 - London: Collins, 1960, Lectures IV and V, p.92f.

delved into and absorbed like other great works according to our personal needs and interests. But we need no longer allow our lives to be rigidly ruled and dominated by them, nor be a party to their conflicts.

As far as a new religion is concerned, its mere invention entails that it must differentiate itself from other religions. Being a religion means that it claims to have the ultimate answer which need not be sought anywhere else. Those who belong to it, form an élite who consider themselves superior to or distinct from the rest of humankind because they know what everyone else does not know. The fact that they fail to convert everyone else to their way of thinking only increases their isolation and sense of superiority. As they become increasingly cut off from reality, their reasonings become circular. They conclude that they are different because they are superior and that they are superior because they are different. They lack an outside agency by which their reasonings may be scrutinised and criticised to bring them down-to-earth. Thus, there can never be any overall agreement between religions because there is nothing over and above them all so that they may be judged relative to each other.

> Religions are cut off from one another by barriers of mutual incomprehension; one of the principal causes of this appears to be that the sense of the absolute stands on a different plane in each of them, so that what would seem to be points of comparison often prove not to be.[4]

Their mutual incomprehension and the absolute nature of their stance in relation to each other makes religion the very antithesis of scientific endeavour which strives for a common understanding of specific problems throughout a community of inquirers. So far from adopting an absolutist stance, scientists usually consider themselves to be servants of truth and humanity rather than servants of a God who is beyond humanity and all human notions of truth. They are therefore fully aware of the extent to which they are prone to human error and misconception and do not regard themselves to be the repositories of absolute God-given truths.

During this century, attempts to reform religion have gone in either of two directions: (1) towards liberalisation and secularisation; (2) towards fundamentalism and literalism. The former offers compromises that religion cannot accept and the latter drives it back to its repressive past. The latter is the most recent development, but neither development is enough to revive

---

[4]   Frithjof Schuon, *Gnosis: Divine Wisdom*, London: John Murray, 1959, p.11.

religion in the face of the overwhelming success of science in explaining more and more about life and the universe we live in.

Admittedly, it is better to have a religious belief of some kind than have no belief in anything at all. But it is better still to have beliefs that make sense and do not require a suspension of common sense and an overlooking of scientific evidence. While there is no intention here to arbitrarily deprive anyone of their own religious views, it is already obvious that religion in any formal sense is now out-of-step with the society we now live in. It is outdated in the first place because it is increasingly no longer needed. We have developed much better ways of dealing with the unknown and unfathomable aspects of our lives. The answers of the scientists are more interesting, profound, and ultimately more satisfying than the old myths which religion only has to offer. Black holes, for instance, are as difficult and unfathomable for the layman to understand as any resurrection myth but there is always the possibility of understanding them better as the evidence grows of their existence and their properties. But with regard to religious myths and mysteries, no further evidence or further elucidation can make any more sense of them. They are to be accepted entirely as they are given, whether they insult our intelligence or not.

Religious thought is too rooted in pre-scientific concepts to make further progress in the face of the undeniable progress of science in making sense of the universe. Religious pre-occupation with proving the existence of God, its introspective wrestling with sin, its self-destructive positing of evil as being the direct opposite of good, are all examples of dead-end problems that impede the moral and spiritual progress of intelligent beings rather than contributing to it. Its obsession with outmoded problems of this kind mean that religion is more retrospective than science. The latter's discoveries enable intelligent beings to look forward to the future with some confidence concerning what they can do in the future; whereas the former's obsessions destroy self-confidence and self-esteem. They may actually prevent individuals from making as much of their lives as they are capable of doing.

By and large, religion represents a backward-looking failure to come to terms with the future. For the omnipotent capacities of God can now be seen as an idealisation of the future potential of intelligent beings in the universe. Moreover, amidst all the implausible histories and myths, there is also packed into the conception of God everything that intelligent beings could do in the universe, provided they continue to make progress in realising their potentialities in the future.

Thus, Teilhard de Chardin[5] unintentionally obviated the need for religion when he re-oriented his view of God from the past towards the future. Our thoughts of God become no more than intimations of what intelligent beings might be able to accomplish in the future. All that the ontological proof for the existence of God achieves is to show the possibility of things becoming better in the future **because** of the existence of our highest ideals of perfectibility and infinite capacity. In that view, God is a **prospective** notion that leads us forward into the future, where also lies the noumena or ultimate reality of things. But the notion itself is out-of-date and belongs to a different kind of society than the one in which we now live. Indeed, if Jesus Christ were to witness the conditions in which most of us now live, he would doubtless think that the Kingdom of Heaven had now been achieved here on Earth. Our living conditions are generally far beyond anything he could have imagined in his day. And he would doubtless be amazed to find that his message was still considered by some to be relevant to everyday life today.

In emphasising the past, religion is of decreasing relevance to present-day society. Its emphasis on ritual, liturgy, and homage to non-existent beings indicates that it represents the playful rather than the practical propensities of humankind. Primitive man's response to the unknown and the fear that it engenders, is to hide behind make-believe, myths, fairy tales, and ritualistic ceremonies that may be representative of realities but provide no practical means of coping with these realities.

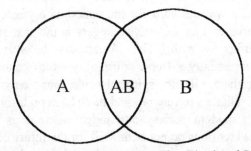

Figure One: The Relationship between Play, Ritual and Science

Where A = play, fun, and games.
AB = ritual, ceremony, liturgy.
B = purposeful activity.
B - A = purposeful activity based on empirical knowledge and evidence.

[5] In works such as *The Phenomenon of Man*. See Chapter Six of this book.

In so far as religion involves ritual and ceremony, it is an intermediate activity which incorporates play and fun on the one hand and purposeful activity on the other hand.[6]   But it lacks the basis of empirical knowledge and evidence which characterises science. Religion thus incorporates senseless irrationality in so far as it is not based on empirical knowledge and evidence which alone enable us to fulfil our goals realistically and predictably. It therefore perpetuates irrational thought and belief because it provides no way of bringing these under scientific scrutiny without destroying the very faith and unreason on which they themselves are built. Hence the tensions created by attempts to rationalise the resurrection myth in Christianity, as fundamentalists rightly see any attempt to modernise the Christian view as being a direct threat to their faith.

A science of the human spirit, however, has the purpose of bringing the puzzling, paradoxical and irrational aspects of life under scrutiny; not necessarily a purely scientific scrutiny, but one of an explicit and above-board nature in which nothing is regarded as esoteric or inaccessible to the public or 'unbelievers'. Its use of evaluators, namely, the universal notions, the noosphere, and posterity, provides it with overall standards which comprehend the human race as a whole and which are not tied down to the narrow views of a self-serving religious élite.

Religion impedes the progress of humankind towards a society that knows where it is going in place of one that waits for God-given inspiration and gets nowhere in the process. The United States of America is an example of a nation which has recently reverted to God worship because it has failed collectively to find a way forward for the nation as a whole. Its progress is now entirely material and its spirituality lingers in the past and is apparently incapable of further growth. The Americans balance their extreme materialism with an equally extreme spirituality which cannot be reconciled with that materialism. Their spiritual side has only the outdated, backward-looking religions to rely on, and these have no lasting answers as to how to cope with modern society and judge where it is taking us. The resulting unresolved tensions do not bode well for the future of such a nation.

The USA's material prosperity makes it the richest and most economically advanced country in the world. But its spirtual barrenness is revealed in the failure to give the world the cultural leadership it deserves, to bring the nation together, and eliminate its own social problems such as poverty, homelessness, racial tension, violence, and anti-government feeling. It may be

---

6   This argument is suggested by some passages in Johann Huizinga's book, *Homo Ludens*, London: Granada Publishing, 1970: for example, p.36f.

advancing materially but it appears to be regressing culturally in its harking back to worn-out religious solutions, as for instance in the case of the recent 'Promise Keepers' movement which resurrects Old Testament values. This development is worrying even though the movement is benign and polite at the moment. It is not improbable that it will be taken over by fanatical extremists who will arm the movement and invade other parts of the world in the cause of religion. Such a latter-day crusade is an alarming possibility because of the uncritical dogmatism which underlies such religious movements. There is more on this in the next section.

The only workable answer to the problem of reasserting our spiritual side is the humanist one being worked out here which fully accepts the scientific view and interprets the human spirit from that point of view. In this way, the complications of the Information Technology society evolving before our eyes may be made sense of, consolidated and made the basis of real and lasting progress for the whole human race. Any other way involves the arrogant imposition of dogmatic and bigoted solutions which delimit people instead of allowing them to find their own way out of their problems.

Though religion is outdated and ought to be superseded by something better, this does not necessarily imply that every aspect of religion is to be uprooted, discarded, or dismissed. What is valuable about the achievements of past religions is often well worth preserving and should be made use of. Many magnificent cathedrals, temples, and churches are an admirable contribution to our civilisation. Similarly, religious music and hymns are not only venerable but often moving and inspiring. Thus, whatever replaces religion has the duty and responsibility to preserve and make use of everything that is good and valuable about our religious endowment. Otherwise, it will not be a worthy successor but only a means of obtaining change for change's sake. Above all, whatever replaces religion should be a vehicle for taking civilisation to greater heights, and this can only be done by doing as much justice to the past as will make it worthy of the future.

2   Why Believe in God at all?

> There is nothing harder, than to bring a man to a perfect
> understanding of himself: what a vile, haughty, and base creature he
> is–how defiled and desperately wicked his nature–how abominable
> his actions; in a word, what a compound of darkness and wickedness
> he is–a heap of defiled dust, and a mass of confusion–a sink of
> impiety and iniquity, *even the best of mankind*, those of the rarest
> and most refined extraction, *take them at their best estate.*
>
> Binning's Sermons.[7]

The above quotation represents misanthropic Calvinism at its most
objectionable. In its context, the writer, Hugh Binning (1627-1653), thinks
that self-knowledge can only be of the very worst side of our natures. In his
view, the aim of religion is to humble and demean people, not to uplift and
enlighten them.

> Now, I say, here is the great business of religion, - to bring a man
> to the clear discerning of his own nature, - to represent unto him
> justly his own image, as it is painted in the word of God, and
> presented in the glass of the law; and so by such a monstrous
> appearance, to affect his heart to self-abhorrency in dust and ashes.[8]

This leads to the vital question: why should we bother believing in God at all,
if in comparing ourselves with him or her we merely demean and degrade
ourselves? Is there any purpose to be served in worshipping a being that does
nothing for us except make us lose all confidence in ourselves? Why believe
in God if he manifestly does not believe in us as beings independent of our

---

[7]   *The Works of the Rev. Hugh Binning*, Edinburgh: William Whyte, 1840, Vol. II, p.302.
This passage was partly quoted by H.T. Buckle, in his *History of Civilisation in England*,
1861- London: Henry Frowde, 1906, Vol. III, ch. IV, 'An Examination of the Scotch Intellect
during the Seventeenth Century', p.259, fn 503, as evidence for his opinion that 'the Scotch
Kirk' at the height of its power in the seventeenth century was second only to the Spanish
Inquisition in its intolerance, bigotry and cruelty (cf. *op. cit.*, p.278).

[8]   *Ibid.* Binning was a brilliant scholar who at the age of 19 became regent and professor
of philosophy at Glasgow College, before becoming minister at Govan. His brilliance came
to the attention of Oliver Cromwell who, on 21st April 1651, attempted to convert the
Glasgow clergy to his brand of religion. Binning defeated Cromwell's ministers in debate
and moved Cromwell to menacingly clasp his sword and say: "This young man has
everything tied up, but this will loose all again." This illustrates how religious people tend
to reach for their weapons when faced with contrary arguments.

belief in him or her? The answer to such questions must be that we can well do without believing in the existence of such a being.

God belief leads quite naturally to Calvinistic extremes of self-abhorrence when the deity becomes the object of unalloyed and fundamentalist worship by those who value it more than themselves and the human race at large. How such extremes are reached, can be shown by reference to scripture; first of all, to the story of the Tower of Babel:

> And the Lord came down to see the city and the tower, which the children of men builded. And the Lord said, Behold, the people *is* one, and they have all one language; and this they begin to do: and now nothing will be restrained from them, which they have imagined to do. Go to, let us go down, and there confound their language, that they may not understand one another's speech. So the Lord scattered them abroad from thence upon the face of all the earth: and they left off to build the city.[9]

No explanation is given us in the above passage as to why it was so necessary to 'restrain' people from doing what 'they have imagined to do' but the implication is that human beings are not deserving of such liberties which are only worthy of the majesty of God. This exemplifies how god belief prevents people doing anything at all which will distinguish them and justify their existence on this planet. It does so by demeaning the human race so that they are discouraged from doing anything that might meet with God's displeasure. This turns out to be anything and everything that people can think of doing which has any consequences at all.

Another example of this demeaning of man lies in the overweening jealousy of the Old Testament God: 'Thus saith the Lord; Cursed be the man that trusteth in man, ...Blessed is the man that trusteth in the Lord, and whose hope the Lord is.'[10] Mere humans are not allowed to trust each other, since only God is deserving of such trust. This attitude means that the man of God cannot enter into meaningful relationships with other people without compromising his exclusive relationship with God. The concepts of human society and sociability are incompatible with this attitude since they depend on the maintenance of trust and understanding between people.

Even the more loving God of the New Testament demands inhuman and unworldly devotion by attributing worldly things to the devil in the notorious temptation scene allegedly undergone by Christ:

---

9 Genesis, ch. 12, verses 5-8.
10 Jeremiah, ch. 17, verses 5 and 7.

> Again the devil taketh him up into an exceeding high mountain,
> and shewth him all the kingdoms of the world, and the glory of
> them; And saith unto him, All these things will I give thee, if thou
> wilt fall down and worship me.[11]

The devil offers Christ three temptations in this scene and his rejection of these have done no service to humankind, least of all to the Christian authorities who had to 'correct his work' in that regard, as Dostoyevsky pointed out in his famous 'Grand Inquisitor' passage in the novel, *The Brothers Karamazov.*[12] But, according to Dostoyevsky's Grand Inquisitor, the authorities corrected the effects of this unwordliness by appealing to 'miracle, mystery, and authority'.[13] Lies and deception were thought by him to be necessary to keep people contented with their lot in life. In fact, contrary to the Grand Inquisitor's view, the lies and deception were necessary because of the inadequacies of religious belief which demanded acquiescence in the absurd and irrational. These inadequacies arose because of the inhuman demands of god belief. As the notion of an all-perfect God demands that human beings refrain from bettering themselves, they have to be kept in their place by indoctrinating them with absurd and irrational beliefs which confuse them and cause them to lose confidence in their own reasoning powers. On the contrary, when we have faith in each other's abilities then we can trust one another with the truth. It is only when we cheapen each other by comparing our weaknesses with the perfection of God, that trust between people is lost, and truth is the first casualty.

Furthermore, it is self-defeating to attribute to the devil everything that is most human about us, since it is then difficult to find anything divine in our attitudes and behaviour. In contrast, it is by working within our human limitations that we excel ourselves and aspire towards divine attributes. God gets in the way of our justifiable aspirations in that regard. In exceeding our

---

[11]   Matthew, ch. 4, verses 7-8.

[12]   Fyodor Dostoyevsky, *The Brothers Karamazov*, 1880 - London: Penguin, 1985, pp.291-305. The same message was more succinctly expressed in the 18th century by the Scottish judge, Lord Braxfield, responding to a man whom he had just condemned to hanging for treason at the time of the French Revolution. The man defended himself eloquently by saying that Christ too had been a reformer, to which Braxfield wryly responded: 'Aye, and muckle he made o' that; he was hangit!' This suggests that Braxfield himself would have meted out to Christ the same punishment for much the same reasons as the Grand Inquisitor.

[13]   *Op. cit.*, p.301.

limitations we can make monsters of ourselves e.g. Hitler, Pol Pot and others possessing deluded ideas of what constitutes excellence and superiority.

The claims for God and the absolute subordination of man to God are taken to their ultimate limits in the Koran of the Moslem religion. The sixteenth Sura (the Bee) renders everything whatsoever the work of God, virtually leaving nothing for people to do but worship God. Here is a sample of the ubiquity of God's favours to man:

> 81. It is God Who made.
>   Out of the things He created,
>   Some things to give you shade;
>   Of the hills He made some
>   For your shelter; He made you
>   Garments to protect you
>   From heat, and coats of mail
>   To protect you from
>   Your (mutual) violence.
>   Thus does He complete
>   His favours on you, that
>   You may bow to His will
>   (In Islam).[14]

The Koran also appears to rule out the need for us to seek scientific explanations for the phenomena of the universe. According to the twenty-first Sura (the Prophets), science is literally a form of 'unbelief'. All the explanations we require lie within the book, so that any attempt to correct them or elaborate on them, must indicate a failure to believe in the God-given message:

> 30. Do not the Unbelievers see
>   That the heavens and the earth
>   Were joined together (as one
>   Unit of Creation), before
>   We clove them asunder?
>   We made from water
>   Every living thing. Will they
>   Not then believe?[15]

---

[14] *The Holy Qur'ân*, trans. Abdullah Yusuf Ali, London: The Islamic Foundation, 1975, p.678. This translation seems to capture the poetry and passion of Mohammed's prose in a way that, for instance, the bland Penguin translation fails to do.
[15] *Op. cit.*, p.828.

Thus, according to this view, god belief overrules any other belief whatsoever. Holy scripture already contains all thinking needed for a decent life and no further interpretation is required. Presumably such scriptures were left in the hands of scholars rather than literalist mullahs at the time when Islamic countries led the world in scientific and mathematical thinking, that is to say, during the period of eighth to eleventh centuries AD.

Though Buddhism involves no explicit god belief, it nevertheless takes one aspect of religion, namely meditation, and makes a god of it, in the sense of making it the sole end and business of life. This demeans human beings every bit as much as explicit god belief, as nothing is thereby accomplished to make life better or to secure our future as a species. What is more, its promotion of solitary meditation is the philosophy of a bag person, and if universally adopted, would spell the end of civilisation as we know it:

> One who delights in solitude is content with his own company, eats wherever he may be, lodges anywhere, and wears just anything. To shun familiarity with others, as if they were a thorn in the flesh, shows a sound judgement, and helps to accomplish a useful purpose and to know the taste of a happy tranquility. . . . The solitary man then drinks the nectar of the Deathless, he becomes content in his heart, and he grieves for the world made wretched by its attachment to sense-objects.[16]

Meditation techniques of Buddhism may serve a useful purpose in promoting rest and relaxation. But in general to empty the mind for long periods of time is only to atrophy the brain and ruin one's powers of concentration and mental application.[17]

---

[16] *Buddhist Scriptures*, selected & translated by E. Conze, London: Penguin, 1979, pp.107-108. Anyone who doubts that a promotion of anti-social solitude is not deleterious to civilisation, should consult Colin Turnbull's book, *The Mountain People*, London: Paladin, 1984, which documents the breakdown of social relationships and loss of moral values in a tribe of hunter gatherers. They learnt to live entirely for themselves: 'for the excessive individualism of the Ik, coupled with the solitude and boredom of daily life, did not make for many significant relationships of any kind' and they had little love for one another (*op. cit.* p.196). The Tierra Fuegan peoples described by Darwin in his *Voyage of the Beagle*, were similarly lacking in trust and cooperation between each other. He blames this on 'the perfect equality among the individuals' and suggests the need for property and strong leadership (Ch. X, last paragraph). This says little for the benefits of egalitarian democracy.
[17] It was fashionable in the Sixties to believe that Western thinking used the left hemisphere of the brain and was verbal and analytical, whereas the Eastern thinking right-hemisphere and was creative and holistic. Thus, a balance between these might be achieved. While there may be something of value in this view, it cannot mean adopting

The above passages exemplify the way that religious scriptures undermine our confidence in ourselves and our ability to work towards a better future. Such passages are of course open to a more liberal and enlightened interpretation. But it is the literal and fundamentalist interpretations of the scriptures which has recently been coming to the fore. By adhering to the letter of their scriptures, fundamentalist thinkers are reverting to medieval harshness and insensitivity. This ensures that religion, even today, constitutes an impediment to finding our own way forward because of its crutch-like reliance on God and its suspicion of scientific knowledge in general. In overemphasising our weakness, religious thinking enslaves us to all-powerful external agencies such as God, angels, aliens, demons or whatever. This is precisely the aim of a book by fundamentalist Christians, called *Truth is Stranger Than it Used to be.*[18]

The writers of that book think that it is arrogance on our part to consider ourselves autonomous beings responsible for our own fate. They evidently do not consider it progress that we no longer need to genuflect to a non-existent being who is only allegedly superior to us. But contrary to their view, a sure and certain sign of human progress lies in the fact that such imaginary beings are no longer feared and reverenced by us. Why is this so? Well, the amazing advances in our scientific knowledge make it so. These advances are summed up by the Amazonian tribesman who proudly said that his people no longer feared the Moon as they had been told by white men that it was only a large rock. Fundamentalist Christians apparently wish us to turn the clock back and become as ignorant, fearful and weak as our ancestors. The authors of this book do not say this in so many words but it is the undoubted effect of their arguments. Indeed, they explicitly welcome advances in living standards but only in so far as these are god-given, as if these advances were not solely the result of human effort and enterprise.

The arguments of the first chapter of the book, *Truth is Stranger Than it Used to be,* may be of particular comfort to fundamentalist Christians but these arguments are backward looking and they hardly do us justice as a species. These include an argument against the 'false gods' of scientism, technism, and economism, which looks formidable but it does not bear close examination:

Eastern meditation techniques to the total exclusion of Western thought processes.
[18] J. Richard Middleton and Brian J. Walsh, *Truth is Stranger than it used to be: Biblical Faith in a Postmodern Age,* London: SPCK, 1995.

> **Scientism** . . . corresponds to the modern belief that science
> functions as the omniscient source of revelation in our culture and
> provides us with authoritative knowledge of what is truly important.
> **Technism** . . . corresponds to the modern belief that the
> effective translation of scientific knowledge into power over and
> control of creation provides us with technological omnipotence,
> enabling us to achieve any end we may desire.
> **Economism** . . . corresponds to the modern belief that a rising
> standard of living (defined largely in economicterms) is the ultimate
> goal in human life and the only route to personal happiness and
> social harmony. [19]

But who holds such beliefs? If anyone does, they can only be the most dogmatic and arrogant of individuals who believe uncritically in the omniscience of science, in the omnipotence of technology, or in an unending growth in our standard of living.   In fact, the authors are displaying their ignorance of the way science works. Science is not a religion which anybody adheres to. It is a dynamic community of intellectual and experimental activity in which there is as much disagreement about fundamental things as there is agreement.

The same applies to the other 'isms' mentioned in that quotation. Scientists and academics throughout the world do not hold their beliefs uncritically, and masses of critical papers are being published yearly about the role and effects of science, technology, and the perils of unbridled economic growth. The ongoing debate about such matters ensures that no one in the field is complacent about such matters. But the trouble with dogmatic religious types is that they implicitly believe that everyone else must adhere to beliefs as dogmatically as they do to their own. They are unable to focus on the subtlety of the scientific approach to things which is too flexible and openminded for their mentality.

Dogmatism, after all, consists in being inordinately attached to one's opinions and beliefs to the point of defending them against all contrary arguments or evidence whatsoever. The scientific and humanist view is that no matter how self-evidently true any belief may appear to be, it is still open to review and criticism. This was famously expressed by Karl Popper as the 'falsifiability' of the said belief.[20]   That view also involves the 'rational passions' mentioned in the Introduction. These demand the highest intellectual

---

[19] *Op. cit.,* p.22.

[20] For instance, in *The Logic of Scientific Discovery*, London: Hutchinson, 1968, ch. I, §6, p.40f.

standards as a matter of passionate involvement in a disinterested quest for truth. Thus, dogmatism is treated as a matter for contempt and not just dispassionate disapproval.

Religious faith is essentially dogmatic when it does not allow contradiction or examination of its presuppositions. But the very purpose of its being something held by faith means that contradiction and examination are not tolerated; hence St. Augustine's dictum: *credo quia absurdum* - I believe **because** it is absurd. Any attempt to make religion less dogmatic and more openminded threatens its very rationale i.e. the faith that governs and makes it credible to its adherents. This weakens religion rather than improves it, and a fresh start seems inevitable in view of this.

What is most objectionable about the arguments of these fundamentalist writers is their recurrent reference to the weakness and unfitness of the human race. They want us to be humble in the sight of God, and refrain from meddling in mysteries of the universe since these things belong to God, not man - thus echoing the Catholic Church's interference with Galileo's work. This is how out-of-date they are in their thinking. Such thinking dates back at least to the fourth century, when St. Basil (died 379AD), who in spite of being educated in Athens and acquainted with the works of Aristotle,[21] wrote the following:

> Of what importance is it to know whether the earth is a sphere, a cylinder, a disc, or a concave surface? What is important is to know how I should conduct myself towards myself, towards my fellow man and towards God.

In response, the view of this science of the human spirit is that such scientific knowledge is important because it contributes, firstly, to our self-knowledge in knowing where we stand in the universe, secondly, towards improving our conduct towards people because we know that the human race lives vulnerably on this planet which must be husbanded by us all together regardless of race or creed, and, thirdly, towards making us responsible for our own lives instead of vainly relying on God. Without scientific knowledge we lack self-respect not only as a species but also as individuals finding our place in a vibrant civilisation that seems to be going somewhere in making good, though not perfect, use of that knowledge.

---

[21] Cf. F. Copleston, *A History of Philosophy*, 1950 - Image Books, 1962, Vol. II, ch. 2, p.43.

The writers of the book, *Truth is Stranger*, use the postmodern reaction against modernism to bolster their position. According to them, the modernist faith in human power and dignity has been replaced by postmodernist scepticism of our powers. But this approach is to no avail as the authors are assuming that postmodern movement is an all-encompassing world wide view that reflects the *Zeitgeist*, but it is nothing of the sort. In fact, the scientific view of the world is much more widespread and more generally accepted by the educated public. A few fashionable French philosophers do not make for a great world movement affecting the lives of everyone. They may attract the interest of some intellectuals, while being reviled by many more, including many analytical philosophers. And the great general public knows little and cares less about them.

The real, all-encompassing view is the scientific one, which really does affect the lives of everyone, so that the latest advances in science hit the news regularly whether it is about cloned sheep, vehicles exploring Mars, or whatever. The public hungers and thirsts for the latest news in science, technology and medicine. As a result, the scientific view is powerful enough to resist blows from those have no understanding of the self-critical nature of scientific research. Many scientists worry just as much as the public about the consequences of genetic research and where it is leading us.

The fact is that the power of science now gives us the strength and will to be autonomous, as well as circumspect about the use of our powers. It is time that religious-minded people accepted this state of affairs so that they may also contribute to human well-being in more realistic ways than through the medium of god belief. Hence the importance of this science of the human spirit because it defines that spirit in terms of our purposeful activities, and not as something divine or God-given.

3 The Harmful Nature of the Notion of God

> In order to cure most of the ills of human life, I require not that man should have the wings of the eagle, the swiftness of the stag, the force of the ox, the arms of the lion, the scales of the crocodile or rhinoceros; much less do I demand the sagacity of an angel or cherubim. I am contented to take an increase in one single power or faculty of his soul. Let him be endowed with a greater propensity to industry and labour; a more vigorous spring and activity of mind; a more constant bent to business and application.   David Hume[22]

---

[22] David Hume, *Dialogues Concerning Natural Religion*, 1779 - London: Penguin, 1990, pp.118-119.

Anthropologically speaking, it is generally accepted that humankind lacks the genetic endowments to rival those of other animals, such as those as listed by Hume above. We are a species which is not genetically specialised but is 'generalised in its capacities'.[23] We need to use our intelligence, industry and co-operative powers to survive and thrive. Self-reliance has apparently been bred into us since we emerged as a thinking species. But the notion of God overrides this natural self-reliance by subordinating us to an inhuman and overperfect creator.

This loss of self-reliance did not prevail in the western world until polytheism was eradicated in the Roman Empire during the reign of Theodosius from 378 AD onwards. It is probably no coincidence that the decline of the Western Roman Empire accelerated after the abolition of a polytheism with which people could identify. The totally anthropomorphic gods and goddesses of the Olympian pantheon had all our frailties as well as our strengths. Recounting their imagined activities afforded a pre-scientific method of detecting order and regularity in the workings of nature. Indeed, Irwin in his book, *Classical Thought*, argues that Homer's treatment of the gods and goddesses in the *Iliad* and *Odyssey*, paved the way for the later intellectual advances of the Greeks:

> Zeus decides how much of Achilles' prayers he will grant. Hera, Aphrodite, Poseidon, and Athena, as they appear in both poems, have fixed and intelligent purposes. Natural forces, therefore, do not strike at random, but as a result of the steady purposes and intentions of the gods. In looking for regularity, laws, and order in natural processes, Homer begins a search that dominates Greek – and not only Greek – philosophical and scientific thinking.[24]

The enforcement of the Christian view of God throughout the Roman Empire therefore undermined the self-confidence of an entire society. Within a century or so, all innovative philosophical and scientific thinking was brought to end, and superstition and magic increasingly prevailed in the Dark Ages.

It is hardly surprising that the early Christian church was bedevilled with the problems of showing how this essentially inhuman notion relates to human beings. It led to all the trinitarian problems of showing how God entered into human affairs through the medium of Christ. But until the Emperor Theodosius imposed the view of the Nicæan council by military force

---

23 Peter Farb, *Humankind*, St. Albans: Triad/Panther, 1978, p.17.
24 Terence Irwin, *Classical Thought*, Oxford: OUP, 1989, p.14.

throughout the Roman Empire, there was practically a civil war between the opposing factions of catholic, orthodox, Arian and semi-Arian, according to how they viewed the relationship of God to Christ and the Holy Spirit.[25] There was simply no agreed way of deciding between the competing views.

The situation is no better nowadays when there are the competing views of God held by Protestants, Catholics and other sects within the Christian Church. And these disagreements are compounded by the views espoused by Jews, Moslems and other god believing religions. Even recent attempts, for instance, in the book, *Honest to God*,[26] to dispose of a transcendental, supra-natural view of God have not met with universal approval among the faithful. In short, the notion of God has only been a source of division and conflict among people, and life is altogether simpler and more endurable without it. It has caused people untold grief and anguish which could have been avoided if the notion had been put aside in the first place.

The fact is that the notion of God is no more than a convenient social construct which is relative to time and place. As such, it is to be distinguished from the notion as a real physical possibility of something in the past bringing about the structure of the universe at its outset. The former is a wholly culturally relative phenomenon which formed part of pre-scientific attempts to explain the world in which past peoples found themselves. The latter remains only a possibility because of our lack of total understanding concerning the ultimate nature and beginnings of the universe. It is up to science to examine the possibilities of this physical existence which is an entirely different notion of God as having the powers of human beings exaggerated to omnipotent levels. Science will either show the existence of some prior intelligence in the original makings of the universe or, more likely, it will continue to push back the frontiers of ignorance beyond which there can be more interstices for God to be relegated to. For at this stage it is highly probable that the universe came into existence spontaneously and without the need for any instigator or creator.

Otherwise, the notion of God is not only redundant and unnecessary, it is also dangerous and harmful. It is dangerous because it is irrational and can never be adequately comprehended unless anthropomorphically. Because no

---

[25] The most minute and nit-picking difference between the rival factions was surely that between the supporters of the Catholic or *homoousion* view and that of the semi-Arians, the *homoiousion* view. The one believed that the Father, Son and Holy Ghost consisted of the 'same substance'; the other that they consisted of a 'similar substance'.

[26] John A.T. Robinson, Bishop of Woolwich, *Honest to God*, London: SCM Press, 1963, p.64.

rational agreement can be reached concerning what it is, it is a source of constant disagreement to the point of hatred and enmity between different sects of god believers. The more passionately they believe in their own particular notion, the more they fight and kill each other in defence of their particular beliefs. Since the notion is capable of an infinite variety of distinct interpretations, it is potentially a source of an infinite variety of beliefs, each competing with the others for intellectual attention and passionate adherence.

This partisan nature arises because, unlike the notion of the noosphere for instance, the notion of God is a subject of absolute belief instead of relative and limited belief. It demands an absolute and unqualified adherence because there are no limits to its possible application. In contrast, the notion of the noosphere makes no more demands on us than other abstractions such as 'society', and 'company'. Such abstractions are limited in their application because their activities are subject to basic human rights. Also, they are no better or worse than the people comprising them. In contrast, there are apparently no limits to what an infinitely perfect being such as God can expect of human beings. Hence the immolation and self-mortification of the saint or ascetic.

It is also a harmful notion when used to absolve human beings of their accountability and responsibility for themselves and their own lives. This tendency is characteristic of the immature and unfree person when he seeks security in some parental figure to whom he clings in a childlike fashion. In contrast, the mature and free adult is confident of his own abilities in relation to the opportunities that life gives him. He is thus able to be responsible for himself and his own actions without appealing to any external agency. Part of the maturity of an adult person must consist in being accountable for the whole human race because he acknowledges the unavoidability of belonging to it, for good or ill. He is responsible for the human race in that he is a microcosm who encompasses the universe as a whole. Thus, even if God did exist, we can well do without him. The notion of God has now fulfilled its useful function in taking humanity through that stage of adolescent dependence and uncertainty which preceded the development of scientific and technological knowledge. The latter now gives us power over our own destiny, plus all the responsibilities which accompany that power.

Christian apologists such as Dietrich Bonhoeffer have acknowledged this point of view in saying that we have 'come of age' and no longer need the parental support of God:

> God is teaching us that we must live as men who can get along
> very well without him. . . God allows himself to be edged out of the
> world, and that is exactly the way, the only way, in which he can be
> with us and help us.[27]

But the plain fact is that we can do without him because he never existed in the first place. It is the certainty of the latter conclusion which has led to his being 'edged out'. We do not even need him to allow us to do any 'edging' at all. We are doing it on our own. It casts aspersions on our own achievements to assume that there is a God allowing it all to happen when clearly there is nothing there to stop us doing and thinking what we like.

As for the view that God is to be found in the depths of the human soul, this merely prolongs the fiction rather than justifies it. If this is a device to focus the mind on our perfectability, it is superfluous. The universal notions themselves serve that function much more directly by pinpointing the aspects of perfection to be aimed at.

Karen Armstrong, a former nun, concludes her book, *A History of God,* by saying that the concept of God may be outdated but if we are to substitute it with something else, we must pay attention to the lessons to be had from studying the deep-rooted yearning for God which the history of the subject reveals to us.

> Human beings cannot endure emptiness and desolation; they will
> fill the vacuum by creating a new focus of meaning. The idols of
> fundamentalism are not good substitutes for God; if we are to create
> a vibrant new faith for the twenty-first century, we should, perhaps,
> ponder the history of God for some lessons and warnings. [28]

If the concept can be shown, as it is above, to be not just 'an aberration' but also harmful to the spirit and abilities of human beings then it clearly has no useful role to play in our society.

> Throughout history, men and women have experienced a
> dimension of the spirit that seems to transcend the mundane world.
> Indeed, it is an arresting characteristic of the human mind to be able
> to conceive concepts that go beyond it in this way. [29]

---

[27]   D. Bonhoeffer, *Letters and Papers from Prison*, London: Fontana, 1959, p.122.
[28]   Karen Armstrong, *A History of God*, London: Heineman, 1993, p.457.
[29]   *Op. cit.,* p.6.

But if, as is also argued here, this spiritual dimension can be amply accounted for by a noological outlook then again there is no need to posit the existence of supernatural entities of any kind, especially those that are acknowledged to be fictional.

A great simplification in human affairs is therefore achieved by putting aside the notion of God as having anything to do with us in the universe as it is. Attempting to find a place in the universe for this notion makes things unnecessarily complicated and unfathomable. Great mental contortions are called for in accommodating this notion in the material scheme of things. For example, since Newton marginalised the activities of God in the universe, innumerable writers, from Samuel Clarke and Andrew Baxter onwards, applied immense effort and ingenuity in finding a place for God in the gaps left by the physical sciences. But it is all to no avail. No agreement has ever been reached and the conclusive evidence is still lacking while the almighty obstinately maintains his habitual inscrutability and illusiveness.

Also, there is no need here to deal with proofs for or against the existence of God. It is as easy to prove the existence of God as of any other social or cultural artefact - Santa Claus, inflation, the Euro, or whatever. What matters are the effects and consequences of acting upon such a belief. There cannot be many people who continue writing letters to Santa Claus well into adulthood. People usually grow out of the need to believe in Santa Claus. However, the notion of God remains useful because it gives people a way of bringing more meaning into their lives and because it leads their thinking into a wider dimension. This aspect may now be taken over by the science of human spirit, as is now argued.

4 The Notion of God as a Precursor to Noology

> The more I learned about the history of religion, the more my earlier misgivings were justified. The doctrines that I had accepted without question as a child were indeed man-made, constructed over a long period of time. Science seemed to have disposed of the Creator god and biblical scholars had proved that Jesus had never claimed to be divine. As an epileptic, I had flashes of vision that I knew to be a mere neurological defect; had the visions and raptures of the saints also been a mere mental quirk? Increasingly, God seemed an aberration, something that the human race had outgrown.
>
> Karen Armstrong[30]

---

[30] K. Armstrong, *op. cit.*, p.3.

Nowadays, we may interpret notions such as God, angels, and other transcendent beings as symbols heralding the perfectibility of intelligent beings and the possibility of superior beings evolving from them to become super-intelligent beings with technological powers beyond our current comprehension. In by-gone days, before we acquired the immense technological powers now at our disposal, people could only imagine conditions being considerably better than those they were facing at the time. They projected these imaginings on to gods, angels and spirits, as they had no evolutionary view by which to imagine a better and more intelligent species evolving which would have all powers that they could only dream about. They could not conceive of mere human beings flying through the air, travelling at a 100 miles per hour, seeing moving pictures on a box, reaching out to the moon and stars, and so on. Therefore they thought that only gods or other supernatural beings could possibly do such things.

In ascribing omnipotence, omniscience, and omnipresence to the Deity, people are extrapolating from knowledge of their own limited powers to the possibility of superior beings in the future having more intelligence and greater technological powers than themselves in their own lifetimes. Such superior beings are visualised implicitly as having all the powers and capacities which they knew themselves to lack at the time.

Thus, the notion of God is an imperfect harbinger of the noological point of view. It points vaguely in the direction of noology because of the perfectionism which is contained within it. The appeal to God as being an influence on one's thoughts and deeds, is better considered as a conscious or unconscious reference to a noological point of view which transcends the immediacy of one's selfish impulses and motivations. One is using the word God to refer to something which may be rationalised and elaborated as being the noological point of view.

To think in terms of an absolutely 'perfect' being is to misuse the word 'perfect'. It is a notion which only makes sense within the community of human beings. And it signifies only our ability to imagine ourselves being 'perfect' in certain finite and ultimately attainable ways. If we cannot be as perfect as we imagine we can be at present, then it may be possible in the future for human beings, or more advanced intelligent beings, to become perfect in that sense. Thus, the notion of a perfect, supernatural being is entirely illegitimate and inappropriate. The word makes sense only to human beings in the context of themselves being 'perfect'. It makes no sense to apply outside all human or intelligent contexts whatsoever.

The theological viewpoint has invariably identified rationality with a belief in God. But noology relieves rationality of that connection. It does so by taking the place of God at the focal point of all belief systems. It holds that our best and most transcendent thoughts and acts are centred on such universal concerns as the future of life, the human race, and the universe as a whole. Thus, the aim of noology is secure morality on the foundation of universal notions as discussed in Chapter Five of this book. These notions are even older and more universally applied than the notion of God in the Judaeo-Christian-Muslim tradition. And because they are commonly applied in all languages and are not generally a source of conflict and emnity, these notions are better qualified as the foundation of morality than the notion of God which has undoubtedly been a source of conflict and emnity, and perhaps also of immorality.

It is not God that gives people strength in times of trial, difficulty, sorrow, or whatever. What gives them strength is the fact that they are elevating their concerns to the highest possible level so that they can universalise them and so cope with them better. They may call this highest level by the name of God. But in fact it is the embodiment of universal notions in their conception of God which is doing the elevation and not any physical or spiritual presence of any God. Their divine thoughts may thus be equated with their universal ones. In so elevating their thinking, they are transcending themselves to make their thoughts of greater significance than their earthly roots imply. They may believe that this act consists in making some kind of contact with God. But it is simpler and more realistic to treat the act as being a rationalising of one's feelings of unity with the universe as a whole. We make better sense of what is happening by using the above-mentioned universal terms instead of attributing our most beautiful and significant feelings to an entity whose existence has never been established and whose attributes have never yet been established to the satisfaction of all theologians.

The feeling that God is with you, means only that you are at one with yourself and the universe. You are harmonising your baser and your higher elements so that you are more in tune with the universe. This feeling or state of mind is identified with, or given the name, God. But there is nothing behind the name apart from the feeling or state of mind of being at one with the universe. Thus, according to this view, God is not dead since he never really 'lived' in the first place. The entity implied by the notion is redundant and redolent of a more ignorant and uninformed age than our own. However the notion, as opposed to the entity presupposed by it, may be said to 'live' on in a sense when its worthwhile aspects, such as those mentioned herein, are translated into the universal context in which it alone has any lasting meaning.

The goodness of God refers to the positive aspects of the universe which are creative, organising and complexifying, and to which we contribute. By so contributing we reap the rewards accordingly. Thus, what is positive about the notion of God can be adequately expressed in universal terms. What is negative about that notion is entirely anthropomorphic, since it is being viewed from the human point of view. It is thereby given attributes that are unworthy of an omnipotent, omnipresent, and omniscient being. The attribution of anything less than infinite capacity negates that notion and thus demeans it. It is being loaded with all the imperfections of even the best of finite beings.

The view that 'God is love' is simply a way of referring to one of the unifying tendencies of the universe. Love brings us together with other people and makes us feel at one with them. Thus, the attribution of this love is again superfluous since it is simpler and easier to refer directly to these unifying tendencies rather than posit the existence of some intermediary which contributes nothing to our understanding of the nature of these tendencies. This does not detract from the mysterious and mystical nature of this unifying influence but simplifies our search for understanding of such matters.

Even if there were design in the workings of the universe, this does not presuppose the existence of any God or creator. It means only that the natural workings of the universe through time result from an interplay between chance events and determinable causes. And the design in the universe, if there were one, would make increasing sense in the future, as its workings are better understood. Only the notion of 'a god of the gaps' can be clung to in these circumstances.

Assuming that there is no God here and now, there is still the need to justify the ways to the **universe** to man. We have to show that the workings of the universe produce intelligent beings quite naturally, without any design or purpose, and that it is our responsibility to make what we can of our place in the universe. This task is at least begun in the following Chapters.

PART TWO

AN OUTLINE OF THIS PROPOSED SCIENCE

3   The Nature Of Subjective Thought

Has science ever troubled to look at the world other than from **without** ?
Pierre Teilhard de Chardin [1]

1 The Science of the Human Spirit as a Study of Subjectivity

It is argued here that the exploration of the human spirit can be organised into a science to be learnt and practised by anyone willing to make the effort. This new science focuses on the subjective side of human thinking as opposed to the objective side which has been the basis of the triumph of the physical sciences. It is hoped that this new science will do for subjective thought what the physical sciences have already done for objective thought by bringing it into a state of order, practicality and general acceptability.

Accounting for the subjective side of our nature means describing what we do inside ourselves in response to external stimuli, our feelings, thoughts, and everything else which happens to us, and about us. This assumes that we are both passive in receiving external stimuli and active in responding to them, and that these occurrences are independent of anything we are doing within ourselves. It is therefore necessary to show that there are acts which involve 'doing things within ourselves' in opposition to the objective or physicalist view that there is no real distinction between what is happening inside and outside our bodies, and that both can be described in the same terms.

The argument is that, in common with other living creatures, we have an organised interiority which we are constantly maintaining and asserting, against the intrusion of chaotic and disordered physical events. Subjectivity is what we call our own experience or understanding of our internal organisation *vis à vis* externality or physical reality 'out there'. Objectivity, on the other hand, signifies what we are able to do with objects and not what we are doing within ourselves in relating ourselves to these objects.

---

[1]   *The Phenomenon of Man,* London: Collins, 1959, p.57.

Attempts by Ryle and others to deny the existence of the human spirit or 'the ghost in the machine'[2] are rendered untenable, in the first place, by appealing to the facts of biology. It is simply a fact that biological organisms have an internal, goal-directed activity which is distinct from the physical activity that reductively composes it. And we have spirit within us to the extent that our behaviour is goal-directed. Without such spirit, *The Concept of Mind*, for instance, could never have been written. Other ways in which the distinctiveness of our subjective spirit manifests itself are important issues dealt with below.

Ryle took his cue from Wittgenstein who said that 'the inner process stands in need of outward criteria'.[3] The implication is that nothing can take place inside ourselves without being observable or deducible in some way from these criteria. This means that no one can be said to grieve unless there are floods of tears to demonstrate the existence of such grief. As a result of the prevalence of this philosophical attitude, we now have a whole culture based on the bleeding heart syndrome, that is to say, on the premise that all emotions must be out front, otherwise they cannot be said to exist at all.

It is argued here that there is no rational justification for legislating subjectivity out of existence in the Wittgensteinian manner. The act of doing something in the physical world is a physical matter which, as Wittgenstein put it, 'stands in need of outward criteria'. But the 'inner process' has no such need as it is only accountable from a subjective or self-referential point of view. 'I have now raised my hand' is an account spoken after-the-event. 'I will now proceed to raise my hand' is a subjective intention or goal-set and is therefore a before-the-event account. Even 'I am now in the process of raising my arm' has nothing to do with what is actually going on inside my head, when and if I successfully fulfil that intention. What is really going on in my mind is in fact beyond the capacity of any verbal or scientific account to fully explain because it is subjective and self-referential.

Thus, an account based on self-reference is a non-causal account because it is not sufficient to explain what is actually happening, especially in physical terms. The account gives the reasons why someone does or does not do something but it does not claim that any given set of reasons is the cause of what is or is not done. There may be other reasons in the offing which may be equally or even more relevant in persuading the individual to act or not act.

The source of Wittgenstein's view lies in the works of Schopenhauer, by

---

[2]   Gilbert Ryle, *The Concept of Mind*, London: Penguin, 1968, p.17.
[3]   Wittgenstein, *Philosophical Investigations*, Oxford: Blackwell, 1968, Part I, §580, p.153.

which he was greatly influenced both in his youthful idealism[4] and in compiling his *Tractatus*.[5] His later philosophy also shows Schopenauerian influences in respect of the subject who knows but never can be known.[6] Because the subject can never be known within itself, it requires 'outward criteria' to reveal the existence of its inward ruminations. But the first premise concerning the subject's lack of self-knowledge is never questioned but merely tacitly assumed by Wittgenstein. He will not allow us to be aware of our own experiences as something entirely private to ourselves. Furthermore, this unexamined presupposition originates in Schopenhauer's oriental influences, especially in the view that subject does not exist in space and time, which is inspired by the mysticism of the Hindu classic, *Upanishad*:

> It is not to be seen: it sees everything; it is not to be heard: it hears everything; it is not to be recognised: it recognises everything.[7]

Therefore, the origin of Wittgenstein's denial of the existence of introspective activity lies in oriental mysticism and not in any conclusive or convincing thought on the matter. It is an assumption that perhaps makes more sense in its proper context of Eastern philosophy than in its arbitrary import into Western thought.

However, this abolition of the privacy of the subject suited the objectivist programme which consists in reducing all mental events to physical ones. Such is the prominence of this objectivist viewpoint that no one can be said to have any kind of emotion such as pain unless it can be shown that their brain functions are altered as result.[8] The fact that we can look into ourselves to ascertain how we feel is ignored from the start. But ascertaining the nature of such introspection requires a   discussion about the dualistic distinction between subjectivity and objectivity.

---

[4]   Cf. G.H. von Wright's 'Biographical Sketch' in *Ludwig Wittgenstein: A Memoir*, London: OUP, 1962, p.5.

[5]   Cf. Ray Monk, *Ludwig Wittgenstein: The Duty of Genius*, London: Vintage, 1991, pp.143-144.

[6]   Schopenhauer, *The World as Will and Representation*, 1844 - New York: Dover Publications, 1969, Vol. I, p.5. It seems extraordinary that Schopenhauer should begin his book denying that the subject can be known, and yet spends much of his work, and especially the second volume, showing how well the will of the subject can be understood through introspection, thus paving the way for Freud's account of the unconscious.

[7]   Schopenhauer, *The Fourfold Root of the Principle of Sufficient Reason*, 1847 - La Salle, Illinois, 1974, p.208.

[8]   Cf. Saul Kripke, *Naming and Necessity*, Oxford: Blackwell, 1980, p.148.

2 Subjectivity and Objectivity

> As Wordsworth walked, filled with his strange inner joy,
> responsive thus to the secret life of nature around him, his rural
> neighbours, tightly and narrowly intent upon their own affairs, their
> crops and lambs and fences, must have thought him a very
> insignificant and foolish personage. It surely never occurred to any
> one of them to wonder what was going on inside of *him* or what it
> might be worth. And yet that inner life of his carried the burthen of a
> significance that has fed the souls of others, and fills them to this
> day with inner joy.   William James[9]

The dualism being described here is one of an active spirit operating solely within its material basis.   It goes beyond the simplistic dualism of philosophers, such as Descartes, who reduced it to a matter of distinguishing mind from matter, or mental events from physical events, and vice versa. They have merely subordinated subjectivity to objectivity, as if   the exploration of the former were ultimately the preserve of the latter. But it is argued here, that there is no point in distinguishing the one from the other in any absolute terms as they are so inextricably bound together.

The dualism referred to here is richer and ultimately more unfathomable than the Cartesian position, since, for instance, it includes a kind of monism within the dualism. The constancy of the interaction between interiority and externality is one key to understanding this dualism. Though researchers in the field, such as neurophysiologists and psychologists, tirelessly explicate the nature of this interaction, it is a never-ending task, since a complete understanding of its nature may be approached but never arrived at. Impatiently seeking to establish its nature, once and for all, leads us inevitably to favour one side of the dualistic divide over the other. A well-balanced mind is neither exclusively materialist nor exclusively spiritualist, but an overwrought or oversceptical mind may lurch to one extreme or other since it is looking for absolute certainties where none are to be expected.

Ignoring this dualism in favour of an entirely physicalist view of the universe has given science a lop-sided and inadequate view of the place of human beings and living things in the universe. As Teilhard de Chardin pointed out (see the quotation at the head of this chapter), everything has been interpreted from the outside of things, and the nature of interiority has been ignored. It is argued here that a balanced view requires us to give equal

---

[9]   William James, 'On a Certain Blindness in Human Beings', *Selected Papers on Philosophy*, 1915, London: Dent, 1967, p.11.

weight to these points of view. Because this opposition has traditionally consisted of a conflict between science and religion, the failure of the one to appreciate the point of view of the other has made equality of treatment impossible. The one has alternately asserted itself over the other, and the resultant impasse between them has been behind much of the irrational conflict, hatred, and emnity between European peoples during the last two thousand years or so. It is argued here, that we may eliminate this irreconcilable antagonism only by formulating a science of the human spirit which adopts the methods and attitudes of science while being distinct from the physical sciences as such.

From Descartes onwards, philosophers have attempted to objectify the human spirit to bring it into line with the physical sciences. Descartes treated the mind as a substance as if it comprised objects like those of external reality. He thought that knowledge could be securely founded on these objects of subjective experience, namely, our ideas of things. These ideas are treated as modes of thought and therefore as intermediary between the subject and external reality. They are ambiguously objects of the mind that refer to or represent things 'out there' instead of being that which they are immediately apprehended to be in themselves.[10] Descartes took this view because he was over-impressed, for instance, by the way numbers can be manipulated in the mind: six is twice three, and there is the same proportion between six and three as between six and twelve, and so on.[11] But this involves analysis and deduction in relation to given objects. Knowledge is also arrived at by synthesis and induction which provide us with a holistic and all-encompassing view of objects in relation to what we aim to do with them.

It is argued here that subjective **goal-setting** also supplies the foundations of knowledge, and not just subjective experience and its contents. The last named are entertained in our experiencing of them, but their value and reliability depends not just on our experience of things but on the goal-setting activity involved in experiencing them. What we aim to do in constantly referring to things and in constantly revising our accounts of them, secures

---

[10] Cf. Descartes, *Meditations on First Philosophy*, 1641- trans. J. Cottingham - Cambridge: CUP, 1986, Third Meditation 41, p.28, etc. This view led both to Locke's 'way of ideas' and to Thomas Reid's confutation of 'the theory of ideas' which he regarded as the chief merit of his philosophy, to have 'called in question the common theory of ideas, or images of things in the mind, being the only objects of thought.' (*Reid's Works*, ed. Sir W. Hamilton, Letter to Dr. Gregory, p.88a.) He supplied instead a theory of direct perception which accounts for our direct apprehension of objects.

[11] Descartes, 'Rules for the Direction of the Mind', *Key Philosophical Writings*, trans. E.S. Haldane & G.T.R. Ross - Ware: Wordsworth, 1997, Rule Six 384, p.20.

the foundations of our knowledge in any given situation and gives continuity to our thoughts, words and deeds. Such goal-setting acts serve to unify the mind in relation to its objects so that we are able to put aside information which is not germane to our immediate purposes while we remain reasonably constant to our overall aims and goals. Our knowledge is built up over a period of time because of this goal-setting activity, whereas it is only deconstructed by means of deductive and analytical methods.

Thus, according to this view, the human spirit consists in any goal-fulfilling activity in which meaning and value are conferred on intentional objects. Our spiritual activity is also expanded greatly by noospheric connections and by its reference to posterity i.e. to goals having future consequences. There are therefore five components of this spiritual activity, namely: (1) goal-setting; (2) conferring meaning and value; (3) having an intentional object; (4) being noospheric; and, (5) contributing to posterity in the future. What unifies these components is the self-referential nature of spiritual activity, as is argued at greater length in section three.

This teleological approach to subjectivity contrasts with the ontological approach of such idealists and rationalists as Hegel, Kierkegaard, and the Existentialists. They were concerned more with characterising the nature of existence and of existents than with what we aim to do in making use of them. Their thinking was still dominated by the permanence of Platonic forms which preclude flexible thought concerning the application of universal notions and the content of existents. Thus, even Heidegger was overimpressed by the beingness of things and undervalued the subjective activity involved in putting us in touch with existents and in altering our perspective of them. He reduced everything to one perspective, namely, that of *Dasein*,[12] whereas there are as many perspectives as there are 'forms of life', to use Wittgenstein's expression.

For instance, the very existence of subatomic particles depends on our adopting a scientific perspective since they cannot be directly observed or witnessed. The choice of perspective which we adopt is a subjective matter which depends on our goals, aims, motivations, and desires. And the chosen perspective determines what is apprehended to exist and is therefore a prerequisite to perceiving or conceiving anything to exist.

In focusing on ends and goals, we avoid the reliance of continental idealists on the absolute nature of existence and its forms and arrive at a dynamic view of universal notions which are treated as provisional, open-

---

[12]   Martin Heidegger, *Being and Time*, 1927 - Oxford: Blackwell, 1987, p.67.

ended and on-going, instead of being dictated by clear-cut and definitive logical distinctions, concreted for all time. This ensures that the science of the human spirit engages in synthesis as much as in analysis and is holistic as well as analytical in its approach to the problems dealt with here. For such notions are no longer ends in themselves in our thinking processes but comprise means to ends which are over-and-above the implementation of any dogmatic idea or ideal. For example, the notion of race is not allowed to become more important than the right of anyone to fulfil their legitimate ends as human beings. Nor is the notion of human being allowed to dictate to anyone when or whether they are or are not being human.

The consequences of the objectifying attempts initiated by Descartes may be illustrated by reference to Nagel's book, *The View from Nowhere*, in which the subjective self seemingly has no place in a 'centreless' and objective universe.[13] This kind of view leads Nagel to proclaim the ultimate senselessness of life since there is nothing in life but an unfocused and aimless rambling among the objects of material existence. In a later work, he says that to him 'it wouldn't matter if I didn't exist at all, or if I didn't care about anything. But I do. That's all there is to it.'[14] 'Life may be not only meaningless but absurd.'[15] In response, one can ask how does he **know** this? The fact is that there is no way of knowing this for certain, either by proof or evidence. It is a case of thinking it and believing it - if it suits us. We have as much right and justification to take the diametrically opposite view and proclaim that life is entirely meaningful, if only because we are here to give meaning to it. It is a matter of the **attitude** or personal perspective[16] which one adopts. If we are too lazy and selfish to care about anything, or if we can find no better *Weltanschauung* than Nietzschean nihilism, we will doubtless find Nagel's attitude congenial. The fact that such an attitude gets us nowhere in life will not matter either. As life isn't worth living at all, annihilation, suicide and mass murder seem to be the obvious end-products of **that** attitude if it is sustained long enough and kept to oneself.

So pervasive is the public expression of this pessimistic attitude concerning our future prospects that even humanist writers are prepared to countenance it. Thus, Paul Kurtz, for example, says the following:

---

13 Thomas Nagel, *The View from Nowhere*. Oxford: OUP, 1986, p.61.
14 Thomas Nagel, *What Does It All Mean?* Oxford: OUP, 1987, pp.100-101.
15 *Ibid*. p.101.
16 An attitude in this context is therefore the adoption of a perspective, or way of looking at things, which is peculiar to the individual at one particular time and place, and which is not necessarily shared with, or understood by, anyone else.

> Since the human species has no fixed essence or no ultimate
> purpose, human beings are condemned, to paraphrase Sartre, to
> create who and what they will be at any moment in the future, and
> we are not certain that the future will not be awful. [17]

In using such negative terms, Kurtz undermines his basic message that the humanist view gives us the opportunity and responsibility to make something of ourselves if we so wish. We should dismiss the fatalistic view of the existentialists that we are 'condemned' or thrown into the world to do so. We can choose willingly to take up such burdens or leave them aside. It is a matter of finding reasons and answers within ourselves so that we make up our minds individually and collectively to create a future worthy of our highest ideals. The future need not be 'awful' provided we work together and plan things well enough to ensure that it will be better than it looks like becoming at present.

The present state of the human race always looks dire when we examine it closely and sees only the chaos of everyday living. Just as the activities of the anthill make no sense to the ants living within it,[18] so those who cannot understand the overall workings of human society can make little sense of the apparently random activities they see around them. The notion of the noosphere is one of the ways in which a more holistic understanding of human activities may be achieved. Such an understanding enables us to see our own lives and those of others in a more realistic and rationalistic perspective, since we all have a role to play in bringing value and meaning into being which would not exist if we did not exist. For the contribution of value and meaning is not towards the objective world of things, as the objectivist thinkers assume, but remains within the realm of subjective activity which is unified in terms of noospheric activity when we all share our thoughts by talking to each other.

Because purpose does not exist in the material world, the objectivist thinkers often attempt to legislate purpose out of existence altogether. They reduce or 'translate' purpose into something else. Braithwaite's *Scientific Explanation* and Nagel's *The Structure of Science* contain attempts to do this. Nagel, for instance, reduces teleological statements to non-teleological statements by stating the causal conditions necessary for a biological event or

---

[17]   Paul Kurtz, 'The Evolution of Humanism', *The New Humanist*, Vol. 112, no. 2, August 1997, p.6.

[18]   Cf. Douglas R. Hofstadter, *The Mind's I*, London: Penguin, 1982, p.168f.

function to occur.[19] But a mere restatement of events or functions in another logical form does not legislate purposefulness out of existence. It does not explain the relationship of purpose to the physical sciences; it only side-steps the problem by playing with words. These writers thereby deduce physical statements from teleological ones but fail to account for the emergence of purposeful functions from physical occurrences. This is because they take a purely deductive view of existence and overlook the importance of induction in allowing us to arrive a holistic conclusions. For the act of setting a goal, means looking at things as a whole. It does not require to be justified in terms of physical causes which are the product of theorising about our **physical** connection with the external world and not about our teleological role in it.

It is argued below that in our attempts to find objectivity and causality in the universe we have overlooked the extent to which we bring value and meaning into being in our thinking about things. This is the source of the failure to find a place for ends and purposes in scientific thought. The place for these ends and purposes lies in subjective theory which is quite distinct from physical theory because it deals with what lies within us as unique organic beings. This is first of all made clear by giving an account of the human spirit as a distinctive sphere of activity in its own right.

3 The Activity of the Human Spirit

> The spirit is the true self.
> Cicero[20]

In this context, what is meant by 'the human spirit' is the goal-directed activity in human beings that consists in their intentions, motivations, unconscious wishes, and ulterior motives, which have objects distinct from the people having the intentions, motivations etc. The human spirit is not an entity, life force, or *élan vital* distinct from the physical workings of the brain. It is these very workings which are engaged in purposeful mental activity more or less accessible to consciousness. Nothing more is required to explain the human spirit in reductive terms than the physical laws and theories which have been established by scientists and will doubtless be altered and added to by them in the future. Nevertheless, it is argued here that the workings of the

---

[19] Ernest Nagel, *The Structure of Science*, London: RKP, 1961, p.402f.
[20] Cicero, *De Republica*, vi.16. The original Latin was: *Mens cuiusque is est quisque.*

human spirit are distinct from their material basis because of their self-referential nature.

The human spirit is therefore purposeful mental activity which is specific to each person. It does not originate in external agencies such as God, though the possibility of telepathic communication between human beings is not necessarily ruled out in this definition, provided that a physical and objective basis for such communication can be found. But what is ruled out is 'the holy spirit', envisaged by St. Paul as something independent of human thinking yet which manifests itself in our thoughts.[21] This kind of view reached its ultimate philosophical development in Hegel's view of *Geist* as a kind of 'cosmic spirit' in which we all participate. In reaching self-awareness, we function only as vehicles of *Geist*,[22] rather than positing our own individuality in relation to a chaotically indifferent universe. Though Hegel's motives were philosophical and not religious, his view of spirit nevertheless rationalises the notion of God as being a subjective spirit which manifests itself ultimately in everything.

What makes our mental activity **spiritual,** and hence irreducible to specific brain events, is its goal-directed and self-referential nature i.e. the fact that reasons may be found for the directedness of that activity and that these reasons are the product of an integrated self or person. For the ends of human beings are not just their stated goals, aims and purposes, but also those actual and possible reasons for doing or not doing something, whether these reasons are stated or not, or brought to mind or not. What makes them ends, is the turning in of thought into itself to reach the self as a more or less unified whole. In this way, the spirit is internalised and becomes distinguishable from its externalised workings as a material entity i.e. as a brain or central nervous system. We are not 'centreless' entities but centred upon ourselves. As is argued below, this centring potentially brings us in touch with the universe as a whole.

The formulation of goals, ends, and aims involves a process of reasoning by which both the goal or end and its object are accounted for in the thinking of the goal-seeker. This applies to any act of making up one's mind to do or not to do something, to be or not to be something, to think or feel or not to think or feel. In this way, the spirit relates to objects distinct from itself, and the activity of intentionality takes place. For subjectivity is an activity to be described; it is not a container for discrete objects like those in physical reality. It is the activity in which we relate ourselves, sometimes unwittingly - as goal-seeking entities - to the universe of which we are a part.

---

[21] Cf. I Corinthians 2. 10 - 16.

[22] Cf. Charles Taylor, *Hegel*, Cambridge: CUP, 1977, pp.80-91.

But anything that occurs to a person in the way of thoughts, ideas, images, and feelings, is not indicative of the human spirit unless these objects are actively brought to mind, are consciously attended to, or are the consequence of previous acts of doing something wilfully. I am not spiritually active unless I have a thought before my mind or something occurs to me, or I am looking at something and not just gazing at it inanely. In being so active, I must have some reason for having a thought before my mind, or for entertaining a passing thought, or for looking at something. These reasons comprise the goals or ends for such activity. At the same time, people are not necessarily spiritually active all the time, especially when they do not feel the need to be so.

The spirit thus consists in the active postulation of goals, ends and aims by means of the mental and physical effort necessary to postulate them. Such activity often answers such questions as 'What do I want to do next?', 'What I am thinking of?', 'What did I do yesterday?', 'How do I feel about this or that?' and so on.

The intentional activity of human beings is a spiritual rather than a material affair because of the holistic turning in of consciousness. That a person has the *intention* to wave his hand is something *spiritual* rather than material because the consciousness of having the intention means turning into oneself to make oneself aware of that intention. We acknowledge that it belongs to ourselves because of that conscious awareness. The intention is rationalised thereby and involves a holistic connection with the whole personality. This connecting process comprises the spiritual part of the personality, and it exists over and above any material occurrence in the brain which may be associated with that process. For it is arguable that this activity not only transcends the organism as such but also links the personality with the universe as a whole. This may well occur at the quantum level of existence and it occurs as a result of the holistic nature of the turning in process. The arguments in favour of this view enter into scientific discourse which is beyond the scope of this work, but much of the groundwork has already been done, for instance, by Roger Penrose in his books, *The Emperor's New Mind* and *Shadows of the Mind*.[23]

It is not often recognised by philosophers that goal intentionality is as important as object and meaning intentionality.[24] These three aspects are all

---

[23] See, for instance, *The Emperor's New Mind*, London: Oxford University Press, 1990, p.531f; and *Shadows of the Mind*, London: Oxford University Press, 1995, p.368f.
[24] Cf., for example, John Searle's, *Intentionality: An Essay in the Philosophy of Mind*, Cambridge: CUP, 1983.

indicative of the outward directedness of subjectivity. Object intentionality concerns the wholeness and discreteness of that which subjectivity is directed upon. Meaning intentionality refers to the content of these objects in respect of their similarities and differences with other objects. Goal intentionality is concerned with the purpose which these objects serve from the subject's point of view. It relates the object to the subject and gives the reasons why the object is identified and distinguished by the subject and hence why it has meaning for him. These reasons which we give for our goals and ends, transcend the merely physical and deterministic response to external stimuli. The goal of satisfying our hunger is a reason, expressed or otherwise, which is more than the physiological deprivation which causes it. It is a goal formulated in response to one's feelings of hunger and not to a cellular lack of nourishment. The latter is only a reductionist interpretation of events and does not represent how they are experienced.

Another useful distinction in this context is that between oblique and direct intention.[25] An oblique intention involves mere foresight of the consequences of our actions whereas direct intention consists in setting out to achieve these consequences. The latter requires an act of will to carry out the intention whereas oblique intention is simply a state of mind. It is direct intentions which characterise the activity of the human spirit at its best. But such acts of the will require the involvement of self-reference to make them possible. Unless they refer back to the self as a whole then it cannot be said to belong to the person perpetrating these acts. For self-reference distinguishes our acts from merely mechanical ones, as is now argued.

4 Self-Reference and Subjectivity

> My belief is that the explanations of "emergent" phenomena in our brains - for instance, ideas, hopes, images, analogies, and finally consciousness and free will - are based on a kind of Strange Loop, an interaction between levels in which the top level reaches back down towards the bottom level and influences it, while at the same time being itself determined by the bottom level. In other words, a self-reinforcing "resonance" between different levels. . . The self comes into being at the moment it has the power to reflect itself.
>
> Douglas Hofstadter.[26]

---

25   Cf. Anthony Kenny, *The Metaphysics of Mind*, Oxford: OUP, 1992, p.49.
26   D.R. Hofstadter, *Gödel, Escher, Bach: An Eternal Golden Braid*, London: Penguin 1980, p.709.

Though physical objects may be called 'things', the subject is not a thing but an activity; as is the self, the ego, the will, the soul, consciousness, and every other mental notion of this general sort. These refer not to any particular part of the mind or brain but to mental activity as a whole. Because they are activities, they may not be pinned down, delimited, or defined with any lasting certainty. Any attempt to define them in absolute terms leads to circularity because they are self-referential activities. We cannot refer to them without assuming the existence of what is being referred to. We are only justified in referring to them at all in the context of a theory concerning what we believe ourselves to be doing or not doing within ourselves as opposed to the physical acts we perpetrate in the external world. These processes at least exist within that theoretical context, and the justification of that existence stands or falls with the success or failure of the theory referring to them.

Philosophers are treating these processes as things when they analyse them as nothing but concepts. For example, Armstrong talks of some acts of the will being 'written into the concept of the will'.[27] But he is not really referring to the concept of the will but to the **capabilities** of the will. Thus, a man is not normally capable of raising his body temperature whereas he is normally capable of raising his arm with ease (to use Armstrong's example). The term 'the will' refers to what underlies the acts of a person and it cannot be understood as something to be analysed as if it were a discrete object. It makes sense only in a description of subjective activity.

We are not here analysing the notions of self or will, but describing how they function as processes in rendering us subjectively goal-setting beings. The aim of such descriptions is to show that we have a subjective life distinct from the physical processes which are only observable outside ourselves in external reality. The circularity of these descriptions is unavoidable because our lives are circumscribed and make little sense outside of ourselves and our lives among other human beings. It is up to us to make sense of them within ourselves since nothing else will do so.

In being self-referential in their nature, the self and the will are also holistically active. As processes, they refer back on themselves to make self-awareness possible. In attending to what we are doing in looking, feeling, or thinking about things, we become aware of ourselves as a whole, even if only for a fleeting moment. In being self-conscious in this way, we make an object of the content of subjective activity by turning back into this activity

---

[27] D.M. Armstrong, *A Materialist Theory of the Mind*, London: Routledge, 1993, p.167.

so that the latter is experienced as a whole. Self-consciousness is thus the subject's awareness of its self-referentiality. The self or ego is no more than a reference to the self-referential act itself, and the will refers to the intentional or object-directed activity of the self.

To say 'I did this' means that, in purely subjective terms, an act of self-reference has taken place in which we refer our external act back to the unity of self where it becomes identified with the self. As the latter is not a static thing, the self instantly moves on to other mental or physical occurrences in its self-referential role. The act which has thus been referred back is either stored in one's memory for future reference or forgotten as its occurrence slips from one's consciousness and then from one's short term memory. The unity of self is therefore only momentary and the extent of the unity often varies in response to the degrees of consciousness and attention focussed on the external act.

The object of being conscious is therefore to ensure that this self-reference is constantly occurring to keep ourselves in touch with ourselves. A car driver who finds that he[28] has been driving many miles without being conscious of the fact, has therefore lost consciousness of what he is doing. The automatic nature of the acts that he performs, has made it unnecessary for him to be fully aware of what he is doing. However, the occurrence of an unexpected life-threatening event, such as a vehicle heading towards him, might put his life in jeopardy if he is unable to regain consciousness of what he is doing and react intelligently in response to the situation. A maximum degree of self-awareness seems essential to ensure that our whole range of faculties are brought to bear upon the situation.

The act of self-reference is not here envisaged as a simple interaction between top and bottom levels of the brain, as described by Hofstadter in the quotation at the head of this section. It is seen as an interaction between one part of the self's activities and the self as a whole. This enables us to explain the nature of holistic and inductive thinking in mental terms without presuming to say that this interaction is located in any particular part or parts of the brain.

The physical evidence for the existence of a unifying, self-referential process may consist in the distinction between normal brain activity when we are conscious and self-aware, and normal brain activity when we are not in a state of conscious self-awareness i.e. asleep or in a coma. Comparing these two brain patterns may show up the changes in the overall patterns of brain

---

[28] The masculine gender is deliberately used throughout this book as males in general appear to be in more need of spiritual and philosophical uplift than females.

activity but will not reveal specific areas of the brain where such a process is taking place. Thus, changes in patterns of brain activity, rather than the nature of that activity, may enable us to spot the physical presence of different kinds of subjective activity. But these changes will doubtless differ from one person to another so that nothing useful can be deduced from comparing one person's brain patterns with another's.

. The phrases, 'turning in' and 'self-referential' are therefore metaphors for whatever is occurring physically in the brain when conscious mental acts take place. But they are more than just metaphors in so far as they enable us to understand what we are doing and appreciate the significance of what we are doing inside ourselves when we think, feel, judge, and desire. Their reality of their existence consists in their contribution to self-knowledge.

Similarly, the existence of self, soul, and mind is manifested in their being active not only purposefully but also self-referentially. The constancy of their activity makes them distinctive and ensures their continued identifiability in relation to the physical activity underlying them. Thus, the physical activity in the brain amounts only to a mind when self-reference demonstrably takes place when, for example, a person shows that their expressed feelings and thoughts belong to themselves and to themselves alone. Thus, the evidence for self-referential activity consists in the self being able to identify itself and its distinctive activities. But self-reference itself requires the use of notions such as self, ego, and I, by which we are able to refer to ourselves, so that language usage is a necessary prerequisite to this ability to self-refer. Animals may have consciousness but they have neither minds of their own nor self-consciousness in so far as they lack the language to self-refer.

These self-referential terms such as subject, self, will, and mind, perform an introspective function in enabling us to examine our mental activity in holistic terms. Such introspective activity has no real or beneficial function unless it also helps us to identify those goals and values with which we identify and those with which we don't identify. When our mental activities are goal- and value-related, they are also being externally directed towards objects 'out there'. Therefore, in forming our aims, goals, values and meanings, we regard these as being our own because of the self-referential nature of the activities involved in forming them.

Though self-referential activity is self-contained, it is nevertheless connected with an independent, external reality. If it were not so connected then there would no possibility of correcting and updating its knowledge base in relation to something other than itself. What breaks the self-referential cycle are sensations, feelings and everything that is experienced because our sensory organs and peripheral and central nervous systems are connected with external, physical events. These events are responded to by the subjective system and are used by it to keep the conscious self as completely in a balanced state *vis à vis* external reality as is requisite for the fulfilment of its goals and purposes. What happens is that the self-referential cycle is unravelled by such events as feeling pain, touching something, or looking at an object, and the spiritual energy tied up in the cycle is unleashed to create an act of being aware of pain, touching, or looking at something.

The full account of how perception connects us to external realities is beyond the scope of this book as it takes us into the realms of physical theory.[29] For the account of how the self-referential cycle is broken is largely a physical matter which tells us little or nothing about what we are doing when we form our goals and purposes.

Failure to make this distinction clear has led to an underestimate of the extent to which our thinking about things contributes to the content and quality of the universe. As we shall see, this is particularly the case in regard to the principle of sufficient reason.

5 Subjectivity and the Principle of Sufficient Reason

> The *principle of sufficient reason*, by virtue of which we consider that no fact can be real or existing and no proposition can be true unless there is a sufficient reason, why it should be thus and not otherwise, even though in most cases these reasons cannot be known to us.   Leibniz.[30]

From Leibniz onwards, the principle of sufficient reason has been misleadingly conceived. His view of it, as quoted above, presupposes that reasons are independent things that are found to be the case just as facts and theories are found to be the case. In fact, because we are language users, we are endowed with the capacity to find reasons for anything whatsoever. Thus,

---

[29] Some indication of the theory involved may be found in the the the theory of direct perception as developed by Thomas Reid. As for the reality and independent existence of external objects, one may refer to books such as John Searle's *The Construction of Social Reality*, (London: Penguin, 1996), for the kinds of arguments which are more or less compatible with the view being developed here.

[30] Leibniz, *The Monadology* (1714), as in *Philosophical Writings*, ed. G.H.R. Parkinson - London: J.M. Dent, 1973, §32, p.184.

people can find reasons for believing in the existence of fairies, centaurs, quarks, black holes, or whatever, even though these reasons are not sufficient to convince everyone of their existence or to counter all arguments against their real existence.

The fact is that the universe is completely indifferent as to whether there are reasons for this or that existing or happening. We are the initiators here, and the universe and its contents are the passive objects of our reasoning, speculating, or theorising concerning what is or is not the case. It is only because of our ability to find reasons, explanations, causes, motives or whatever, that the latter come into being and are introduced into the universe of discourse i.e. the noosphere. The stark reality of the universe may impinge itself upon us in no uncertain terms, but it passively awaits our subjective activity in making anything at all of whatever happens to us.

Clarifying the principle of sufficient reason in this way, shows that finding reasons for doing or thinking things is not enough for us. We need to know the aims, goals, perspectives, attitudes, motivations that govern our seeking for reasons and our selection of them. The latter reasons make sense of the content of deeds or thoughts but they don't tell us why these particular deeds or thoughts are chosen and put forward.

This clearly brings subjectivity to the fore instead of its being subordinated to the search for would-be 'objective' reasons for doing or thinking things. The understanding of what is going on in people's minds becomes as important as establishing the nature of things 'out there'. For it follows from these arguments that there are no necessary logical connections which do not result from the subjective selection of reasons for making such connections. The necessity comes from the juxtaposition of reasons and not from the way things really are 'out there'.

It follows also that this clarification of the principle of sufficient reason has important consequences for the problem of causation:

(1) The principle of causation, namely, that every event has a cause is only true in that we can find reasons for the occurrence of anything whatsoever. The cause of anything comprises only those reasons by which we either choose to make the connection between events or find to be sufficient or necessary to make the connection. The principle of causation has nothing to do with reality of nature and everything to do with the power of our intellect or imagination in making connections between events. Thus, we should not be surprised when we find that sometimes there are no such connections to be made in nature, as the realm of quantum physics appears to be telling us.

(2) The use of the term 'cause' therefore implies that we already have reasons, whether adequate or not, for making connections between events. It is not the case that a cause exists to be discovered. We must first of all have the reasons for making the connections and then we believe that the effects are caused, subsequent to having these reasons.

(3) This means that the causes that we ascribe to events do not exist independently of our formulating them. All that exists are the reasons, explanations, theories, laws, and motives, and all these might be indifferently called 'causes'. The term 'cause' is often uninformative since the mere fact that something is conceived to be connected to something else means that the connection is thought to be causal regardless of the quality or veracity of the reasons for making the linkage. Thus, a prevalence of infant deaths in the neighbourhood of a old woman living alone may lead to a causal connection being made by those who believe in witchcraft.

(4) The customary 'cause-effect' relationship is fundamentally inadequate as an account of what is going on. One reason is being mooted for linking the cause to the effect whereas potentially an infinity of reasons and theories may be thought up to justify making the link. What is required is an understanding of the whole range of conditions involved in the linking of events. And this is the purpose of a theory, law, account, description or other generalisations.

(5) More importantly in the present context, nothing is gained by talking of 'mental causes'. (à la Anscombe[31] and Armstrong, for instance). All that exists, are the reasons, motives, and feelings, that we ascribe to mental activity. These might all be said to 'cause' something if something is said to follow from them. Distinguishing them as 'causes' tells us no more than we already know when we refer to them as reasons or motives. That something or other follows from their existence is already included in the act of describing them as reasons, and motives. But what follows from having reasons and motives is not necessarily action or behaviour but the choice, judgment, reasoning etc. whether to do or not do something. Thus, the deterministic threat to our freewill comes from the intrusion of causal language into descriptions of mental activity and not because there is no such thing as freewill.

These arguments show the extent to which subjectivity enters into our causal analyses. How this relationship changes our view of causation and makes the concept of mental cause redundant, is now to be examined.

---

[31] G.E.M. Anscombe, *Intention*, Oxford: Blackwell, 1957, p.16.

6 Subjectivity and Causation

> Those philosophers seem to have had the justest views of nature,
> as well as of the weakness of human understanding, who, giving up
> the pretence of discovering the causes of the operations of nature,
> have applied themselves to discover by observation and experiment,
> the *rules*, or *laws* of nature according to which the phænomena of
> nature are produced.   Thomas Reid.[32]

It is regrettable that in spite of the best efforts of scientifically-inclined philosophers from Bacon onwards, to bury the corpse of causation, it continues to be resurrected by philosophers up to this day. As early as 1620, Bacon argued that the effects are experienced, first and foremost, and then causes are imputed only after we have made something of the effects. The imputation of causation is always the result of inductive reasoning concerning the effects which are experienced or are the result of experiments on the phenomena of nature.[33] More recently, Russell went even further and stated that there are 'no such things' as causes and that 'the law of causality . . . is a relic of a bygone age'.[34]

It is even inaccurate to say, after Hume, 'that the customary conjunction of objects determines their causation'.[35] Unless there is concerted thought accompanying the observation of events which leads to their being conjoined in the mind, then they remain isolated and singular occurrences. There has to be mental activity in which the events are systematically connected in accordance with pre-conceived reasons, conjectures, theories, and motives. The previous assumption was that the conjunction of events somehow preceded or was independent of the act of observing or experiencing them. But when events are said to be causal the said conjunction of events is in fact arbitrarily being selected out of the complex concatenation of events which comprise any complex situation. In thinking of them as causal, the observer is excluding most interconnections to focus on certain isolated interconnections, usually two: the cause and the effect. The latter may be real enough but they are far from being the whole story.

---

[32] Thomas Reid, *Reid's Works*, ed. Sir W. Hamilton, 'Essays on the Active Powers of Man,' p.607a.
[33] Francis Bacon, *Novum Organum*, London: 1620, Book One, §cv & §cxvii.
[34] Bertrand Russell, 'On the Notion of Cause' in *Mysticism and Logic*, (1917), London: Unwin, 1974, ch. IX, p.132.
[35] David Hume, *A Treatise of Human Nature*, 1739 - ed. Nidditch - Oxford: the Clarendon Press, 1978, Book I, Part III, Section XV, p.173.

For example, 'smoking causes cancer' is a wholly misleading statement since it implies a direct and necessary connection between the act of smoking and subsequent cancerous growths. What it really means in broad terms is that the continuous smoking of cigarettes irritates the lungs with carcinogenic substances so that those people susceptible to cancerous growths are much more likely to suffer lung cancer than if they refrained from smoking. In the latter account there is no mention of simple cause and effect. Any adequate account of the connections between events does not identify specific causes or effects but gives an account of the complex influence and counter-influence of some factors on others. Thus, the causal statement is misleading because the evidence suggests that some people who are less susceptible to the growth of cancerous cells may not contract cancer from smoking even if they smoke cigarettes frequently and habitually. Whether their health will be adversely affected in other respects is yet another matter.

Yet the survival among logically-minded philosophers of an Aristotelian quest for establishing necessary and *a priori* connections between things and events, has made them look for causes as if there were such a thing in nature as a causal connection which is not the result of human beings finding reasons for making connections between things. Nowhere is this more so than in the philosophy of the mind where the determination of mental causes is still *de rigueur*.

It is argued here that this outdated quest for causes is the source of all the difficulties in ascribing freewill to the subject. If one is bent upon establishing rigid causal connections between the thinking subject and the external world then there can be no room for freewill. But this overlooks what Davidson has called the 'nomological slack between the mental and the physical'.[36] If we could explain all human behaviour by means of laws and theories, all our lives would be totally predictable and there would be no room for joy and spontaneity. Thus, the physical account of how we interact with the external world can only be approached but never completed without threatening our very humanness.

As subjectivity is both autonomous and anomalous, its interaction with the physical world must constitute a distinct account from that of the subjectivity itself. The interaction is a 'nomological dualism' whereas the subjective account itself is an 'anomalous monism', to use Davidson's terms.[37] The

---

[36]   Donald Davidson, 'Mental Events', in *Essays on Actions and Events*, Oxford: the Clarendon Press, 1982, p.223.
[37]   *Op. cit.*, p.213.

former refers to an interacting process whereas the latter describes a self-referential process.

Davidson, however, believes that he is offering 'a version of the identity theory' even though it 'denies that there can be strict laws connecting the mental and the physical.'[38] This is because he believes that 'some mental events at least are causes or effects of physical events'.[39] But the nomological dualistic account can only make such connections if it has theories or laws by which to make such connections. As we have not yet a coherent account of how the brain works in relation to our subjective experiences, it is presumptuous, to say the least, to assume the existence of such connections. Thus, Davidson's account is defective because his 'anomalous monism' is infected with outdated causal language which tells us little or nothing about what we are really doing inside ourselves.

The language of mental causes is designed to make the analogy between subjective activity and the material world work. It is not designed to tell us anything about what is going on in the mind, as distinct from the physical events occurring in the brain and central nervous system. It therefore assumes from the start what it sets out to prove, namely, that there is no distinction between what is happening in a person's mind and what is happening ostensively in their brain. A *petitio principii* is committed by not discussing the question as to whether subjective activity is distinctive in the first place; it is simply assumed not to be distinctive. As pointed out in the first section of this chapter, Wittgenstein was responsible for this presupposition.

Using the notion of mental cause leads us to underestimate the complexity of subjective activity which is involved in the formulation of goals and purposes. To say that mental causes are involved is to tell us nothing at all except that some acts followed as a result of unseen, internal mental activity. In fact, there is no such thing as an identifiable 'mental cause' of anything we do, think, or say. There are either involuntary physical compulsions that are non-self-referential or voluntary decisions that are consciously entertained because they are self-referential. Subjective activity itself is quite distinct from any description of physical compulsions, reactions, instincts, or unconscious motivations, not because that activity does not involve physical acts but because the descriptions are either after-the-event rationalisations, theorisings or before-the-event intentions, aims, or goals laid down. Both these accounts are in no way identical to what actually happens in our heads

---

[38] *Op. cit.*, p.212.
[39] *Op. cit.*, p.223.

when we subjectively experience anything or decide to think, do, feel, or say anything. In attempting a complete account of these occurrences, we seeking a non-existent pot of gold which may be approached but never reached or grasped. We can only arrive at an account which may or may not serve our purposes for the time being.

The subjective indefiniteness of the causal account arises from the fact that the quest for causes is inevitably governed and delimited by the purposes which we possess *a priori* in looking for them. This contrasts with the disinterested scientific quest for what really exists or for the way things really are. That quest is governed by no preconceived notions except curiosity and truth, whereas the causal quest is hampered by the desire to find the definite causes which will explain everything and make further inquiry superfluous. We know beforehand what we are looking for otherwise we cannot recognise them as being the causes. The scientific view expects the unexpected whereas the causal view is merely confirmed by what are identified as the causes.

These distinctions are important because they enable us to identify more clearly the subjective element in all our thoughts and deeds. What is concerned with our goals and purposes is not objective or factual even when it is disguised in purely causal language. Physicalist thinkers have manifestly failed to make these distinctions and are thereby able rashly to dismiss the existence of immaterial thought processes.

Thus, D.M. Armstrong in his book, *The Materialist Theory of the Mind*, recognises the importance of goal-setting in our thinking but by purely analogical reasoning he arrives at the opposite conclusion concerning the spiritual nature of subjectivity, namely, that there is a physical basis for all subjective activity.[40] In fact, the use of analogies supports the distinctiveness of subjectivity. An analogy only indicates a parallel between mental and physical events. It gives no reason why they should be directly or necessarily connected with each other. However, Armstrong thinks that there is a connection because he uses the uninformative notion of mental causes.

> Purposive activity is a train of activities, initiated and sustained by a mental state, and controlled from beginning to end by perception acting as a feedback cause on the mental state. To put forward a slogan: a purpose is an information-sensitive mental cause.[41]

---

[40]   D.M. Armstrong, *A Materialist Theory of the Mind*, London: Routledge, 1993.
[41]   *Op. cit.*, p.139.

In other words, forming a purpose is caused by the mental state that creates it, and this mental state is identical with the physical events underlying it. But as argued above, he is making the mistake of assigning causes to a mental state which is, by its very nature, a subjective experience being described after-the-event.

Because Armstrong's train of reasoning is entirely deterministic in its nature, it inevitably leaves no room for independent, subjective thought, decision or choice, that is to say, for freewill. However, we are really not caused to do anything in any strict deterministic sense; we make up our minds to do it. And making one's mind up is a decision-making or goal-setting process which may not be reduced to anything except in an after-the-event description. This point is now discussed at greater length in Chapter Four.

4 Purpose, Value and Meaning

> This is the true joy in life: the being used for a purpose recognised
> by yourself as a mighty one; . . the being a force of nature instead of
> a feverish selfish little clod of ailments and grievances complaining
> that the world will not devote itself to making you happy.
>
> George Bernard Shaw.[1]

1 The Holistic Nature of Goal-Seeking

As all our aims, goals and purposes are products of our internal mental
activity, it follows that we are ourselves responsible for bringing these aims,
goals, and purposes into being. For the universe possesses no aims or goals
other than those introduced by living beings which are sufficiently organised
within themselves to generate aims and goals of their own.

The act of setting a goal means intuitively grasping things as a whole. This
grasping consists in taking account of our whole experience of the situation
with which we are confronted. The situation is not being apprehended in
isolation from everything else but is grasped in relation to everything else. It
is a once-and-for-all experience that happens at one particular moment of
time. It has not been repeated in quite the same way at any time in the past
nor will be repeated in the same way in the future.

The uniqueness and all-embracing nature of each goal-setting act is liable
to be overlooked because we are always examining each act in retrospect and
seeing them in isolation from the total situation in which they occurred. But
we are really not capable of reconstructing in our memories the exact
circumstances involved in each goal-setting act. We are liable to subtract or
add too much to our remembrance of the event because we focus on particular
aspects of the event. We are unable to include the circumstances as a whole
because they are potentially infinite in their detailed content.

There is no logical train of thought or reasoning involved in goal-setting
but only a single act of making a decision to do or not to do something or to
think or not to think something. For example, setting myself the goal of

---

[1] George Bernard Shaw, *Man and Superman*, 1903 - London: Penguin, 1971, Epistle
Dedicatory, p.32.

choosing a seat in a restaurant requires me to make up my mind to sit or not to sit in a particular seat. To achieve this, it is necessary to apprehend the whole situation i.e. all the vacant tables, whether I want to sit near a window, whether a particular table will suit my companion, whether any vacant tables are already reserved, and other relevant matters. In general, the more aspects that one is able to take into consideration in arriving at one's decision, the better the decision is likely to be. One has then attempted to eliminate as many errors as possible. Thus, apprehending the whole situation means taking into account as many factors as possible in order to reach the best possible decision, commensurate with the breadth and depth of one's apprehending abilities. Making up one's mind is a holistic activity in which thoughts coalesce into a unified insight of what is or is not to be done, all things considered.

The decision or goal-setting process may be analysed deductively after-the-event but not while it is taking place. The after-the-event reasoning is inevitably selective and is represented in a linear fashion. It is selective because, as already stated, the whole process may not be grasped in its entirety in the exactly the way it is experienced at the time. It is represented in a linear fashion because it is put into a verbal format in which one word follows another in a straight line. As a result, the process, as thus represented in retrospect, loses its holistic unity, complexity and intuitiveness, all of which it possessed at the time of its occurrence.

Thus, a mental act is holistic when it involves not just an object but also a goal, end, purpose or decision which is arrived at in an instant and which embraces as much information concerning its subject-matter as the person is capable of incorporating before setting his goal or making his decision. In that instant, the mind is directed outwards and is at one with its surroundings. The holistic mental act therefore universalises the mind and puts the thinking person in touch with the universe as a whole.

Undoubtedly, reasoning is involved in building up the complete picture on which the goal-setting or decision-making is based. But the actual act of deciding is a holistic and intuitive act. The act of goal-setting thus involves organising all one's reasons around that decision to reinforce and make sense of it. However, the decision can become a dogmatic and doctrinal one when no reasons against it are entertained or are allowed to threaten or undermine it in any way. For the holistic view is just as prone to dogmatism and extremism as its opposite counterpart, the reductionist view.

2 Reconciling Holism and Reductionism

> Both reductionism and holism, if taken as sole guides, lead into a cul-de-sac. 'A rose is a rose is a rose' may be regarded as a holistic statement, but it tells us no more about the rose than the formulae of its chemical constituents. For our inquiry we need a third approach, beyond reductionism and holism, which incorporates the valid aspects of both.
> Arthur Koestler[2]

The fact that all human thought is either inner- or outer-directed is the origin of the distinction between religion and science. Our quest for certainties can lead us in one of two directions: towards a holism which is inner-directed or towards a reductionism which is outer-directed. Either we look inside ourselves to work out what we want to do or to think, or we look outside ourselves to find out what is really the case. Holism involves the formulation of goals through decision-making processes which arrive at unified wholes. Reductionism involves factuality in which things are analysed, acted upon, experimented with to reduce them to their components or constituents. Either we are making wholes and goals out of our experiences, or we are dividing them up, manipulating them, and measuring them to reduce to manageable proportions. Either way we are altering our experiences into something else which is apprehended as bigger or smaller according to the procedure adopted.

Objectivity arises from what is done successfully with objects in the past and present. It does not reside in the objects themselves but in what we are actually able to do to them and with them. An object is something manipulable, whether in the mind or in the physical world and we make something into an object by doing something with it or to it so that it becomes something else as a result of our acts. Thus, looking at a tree as an object means observing something about it, for example, its shape, its species, or its height. It becomes more than it was seen to be at first glance. This view of objectivity as involving manipulable objects is what is here called 'factualist'.

The act of doing something is thus subjective in the decision-making and goal-setting involved in conceiving the act. And the act is objective in what is actually done in or with the act. In the physical sciences, the act involves

---

[2] Arthur Koestler, *Janus: A Summing Up*, 1978 - London: Pan Books, 1983, p.26. Koestler's own attempt at a reconciliation, based on the 'holon', has proved inadequate perhaps because it offers no more than an account of holism and not a way of reconciling it with reductionism.

theorising, measurement, experiment, observation and the like, in the context of scientific activity.

The reductionist and the holistic views only seem to be incompatible because, in isolation from each other, they point in these radically different directions i.e. the one outwardly-directed and the other inwardly-directed. But they are both equally essential to our balanced and purposeful thinking.

The two attitudes of mind have been summarised as follows by Douglas Hofstadter in his book, *Mind's I*:[3]

Hard Scientists	Soft Scientists
Reductionism	Holism
(upward causality)	(downward causality)
+	+
Predictionism	Goalism
(upstream causality)	(downstream causality)
= Mechanism	= Soulism

While reductionism plus predictionism may well equal mechanism, it is disputable whether holism plus goalism necessarily imply soulism. What holism plus goalism imply is the existence of organisms that are internally organised so that they interact with their external environment. This does not imply that this internal organisation amounts to a soul which has an independent existence of its own. It means only that the ability to interact with their environment makes their internal organisation distinctive and relatively independent of that environment. But that organisation is still thoroughly mechanistic and predicable nevertheless. Thus, the distinctiveness and the relative independence of internal organisation is what makes the holism and goalism possible.

There is no evidence to suggest that 'scientists' who adopt one point of view over the other are necessarily any 'softer' or 'harder' than 'scientists' who hold the other one. The distinction is a pejorative one, presumably based on William James's similar one between 'tender-minded' and 'tough-minded'.[4] The favoured viewpoint is assumed to be 'hard' and 'tougher' than the other for purely macho reasons, such as being more powerful, cogent and convincing, so that it is favoured only on prejudicial grounds.

---

3   Douglas R. Hofstadter, *Mind's I*, Penguin,1982, p.197.
4   William James, *Pragmatism and Other Essays*, 1907 - New York: Washington Square Press, 1972, p.9.

The power and cogency of the scientific approach is not being disputed here. The argument is only that the other point of view - that of 'goalism' and 'holism' is equally cogent and powerful. It has its place in the scheme of things and deserves to be developed and applied in its own right.

Goalism is connected to holism in that goals require the whole picture to be brought before one's mind to pinpoint what they are in relation to one's personality as a whole. For they are ultimately related to the needs of the whole organism. They are also brought into being by means of conception and inductive reasoning, and these grasp things as a whole. In conceiving of a goal, one is taking account of the whole situation in the future which is aimed for. To set oneself the goal of completing a certain task within a certain time, one is attempting to grasp the situation realistically and take account of all the factors that might prevent one from achieving that goal. The better one is able to take account of all possible counterfactual circumstances, the more one is going to formulate a realistic and practical goal to be aimed for - something that will work, in other words. Seeing things as a whole means including everything one is cerebrally capable of including within it. One's ability to conceptualise realistically and practically is at least part of what one's intelligence consists in.

Hofstadter and other physicalist writers have not explicitly recognised that these two approaches of reductionism and holism are mutually exclusive ways of interpreting the universe and its contents. Science has been successful by concentrating on the reductionist approach. But holism is an equally valid approach because it refers to the way that wholes are often more than the sum of their parts and include properties which are over-and-above anything to be found in a disparate heap of the same parts. For example, sodium choride has properties quite different from either sodium or chorine.

Computers are based on reductionist principles which cannot take account of the holistic aspect which links biological entities to the universe as a whole. This aspect involves the looping back which Hofstadter refers to. This process links the biological entity ultimately with the universe as a whole. It is the 'implicate order' which Bohm refers to in his book *Wholeness and the Implicate Order*. Each region of space and time has a total order 'enfolded' within it.[5] Each part of the whole contains the order of the whole folded back into it. Thus, the structure of organised entities is already enfolded in the implicate order of its parts.

---

[5]   Cf. David Bohm, *Wholeness and the Implicate Order*, London: RKP, 1981, p.149.

This non-mechanical 'looping back' of holistic structures cannot be emulated on any machine which is based on mechanical, reductive principles. It would have to acquire a biological capacity to do this. In Chapter Three section 4, it was pointed out that self-reference involves a holistic process of apprehending oneself as a whole, and it is this aspect which artificial intelligence would have to recreate to acquire this biological capacity.

Because the biological entity can orient itself holistically in respect of the universe as a whole, it thereby establishes its self-identity *vis-à-vis* the universe as a whole. It may be the case that the self-identity possessed by a human being can only be reproduced by taking account all the cosmic processes in the universe and all the evolutionary processes on Earth. If this is so then we are a long way from having the technology required to do this. It seems indeed to require the omniscience, omnipotence, and omnipresence of a God or infinitely superior being.

Reductionism involves analysing past events to find regularities which can be stated as laws or theories. But the way things and events come together to produce something new and different can never be predicted precisely. This is the inductive problem which Hume first drew attention to. This holistic approach does not solve the inductive problem but gives us a methodology for accounting for it and therefore for coping with it. This is because it is impossible to predict in mathematical or any other terms what will be the precise outcome of any synthesis of parts before that synthesis actually takes place.

> In a non-linear system the whole is much more than the sum
> of its parts, and it cannot be reduced or analysed in terms of simple
> subunits acting together.[6]

This non-linearity makes the future impossible to anticipate with complete certainty. The holistic direction is fundamentally unpredictable, and the future can be planned only within the strict limitations which the reductionist reasoning makes possible.

The extreme tendencies implied by these two viewpoints can be avoided by using the one in conjunction with other. When we attach value and meaning to objects, we use the products of our holistic view to add something more to these objects that they possessed before. But finding out the value of things and what they mean to us very often consists of analysing them and reducing them to simpler components. Thus, in using these two products of our spiritual activity we can achieve a reconciliation of the holistic and

---

6   Paul Davies, *The Cosmic Blueprint*, London: Penguin 1995, p.25.

reductionist viewpoints in terms of what we are intending to do with things, both subjectively and objectively. How this can be done requires an examination of value and meaning with the aim of reconciling these viewpoints in purposeful terms.

3 Value and Meaning

> That it is our opinion which confers value can be seen from those many things which we do not even bother to look at when making our judgements, looking, rather to ourselves: we consider neither their intrinsic qualities nor the uses they can be put to but only what it cost us to procure them - as if that were a part of their substance: in their case value consists not in what they give to us but in what we gave for them.
>
> Michel de Montaigne.[7]

It is argued here that the reasons we find within ourselves for thinking, saying or doing anything give value and meaning to these thoughts, words or deeds. The latter have significance for us because they are ours and because they are something to us. They do not amount to anything of value unless they make sense to us or we identify with them. We add something to our thoughts, sayings and doings in the act of thinking, saying or doing them. And that additional something is the value or meaning they acquire in being thought, said or done by us.

To **value** something is to relate to it personally and bring it into the corpus of important items that make up our personal interests and preoccupations. We relate valuable things to ourselves in respect of our personal interests, such as our worries, feelings, sentiments, opinions, loved ones, and prestige. They therefore **mean** something to us because of that relationship to ourselves. Their meaning at this elementary level consists in our expressing to ourselves something or other concerning them. To that extent, value and meaning are subjective notions applied to reality rather than objective aspects of that reality. They acquire an objective aspect when we actually apply in the external world the decisions and goals arrived at as a result of having put value and meaning on things.

---

[7] Michel de Montaigne, *The Complete Essays*, trans. by M.A. Screech, London: Penguin, 1991. Vol. I, Essay 14, p.66. (Without apparent explanation, Screech has numbered this Essay, 'That the Taste of Good and Evil Things Depends in Large Part on the Opinion We Have of them' as 14, whereas in other editions e.g. the Everyman edition it is number 40.)

As a result, we can say that nothing whatsoever has any meaning, use, or value in the universe except in so far as **WE** put meaning into things, find a use for them, and hence value them. Thus, a stone on the surface of the planet Mars exists independently of our thinking of it and seeing it, but it has no real value or meaning until it is, firstly, thought of by us as existing and, secondly, actually seen by us through the medium of a remote camera, for example.

We are not born or designed to bring value and meaning into the universe, but it is a fact that we can and do so. Our ability to do so is to be exercised for the same reason that a mountain is to be climbed: because it is there. It gives us something to do which we can in fact do and which benefits the universe by enriching its content.

It may be argued that being finite creatures we can comprehend very little of the immensity of the universe in our minds and yet it still has value and meaning even without our intervention. But by that act of comprehending it we are already thinking of that immensity and giving it value and meaning. Unless its possibility occurs to us, it remains nothing to us and to itself. It is not necessary for us to think of **every** particular thing contained within the whole immensity of things, otherwise every molecule, atom and quark possessed by everything would have to be comprehended, and this is clearly an absurd impossibility. Whenever we think of a whole object, we are eliminating its particular content. Thus, we are conferring value and meaning on things because we are comprehending them as wholes, and we cannot do any more than that without absurdity.

We confer value and meaning on things in fulfilling our ends as spiritual beings. Whether or not we were intended by nature to do so is irrelevant since it is a fact that we are clearly able to do so. Anyone who disputes this fact immediately contradicts themselves since the act of disputing it itself brings something meaningful into being which did not exist previously. But how it came about that we introduce meaning in this way is an entirely different question. It is to be dealt with in another account in which our place in the universe is examined.

The chain of events is that we formulate our goals and ends and act in accordance with them. This gives our actions meaning and value which in turn bestow meaning and value on the things acted upon. They all acquire such meaning and value because it is possible to express in words just what that meaning and value consists in. It follows that language is the chief conduit by which we bestow meaning and value on things.

External objects possess, independently of any meaning and value we give them, firstly, the **possibility** of having this meaning and value given to them and, secondly, their permanent existence independently of all our acts of perception and conception concerning them. It is not that they are 'permanent possibilities of sensation' since it is by our acts of perception and conception and by our attending to the objects of these acts that we establish the independent existence of these objects against all practical doubts. Sensation gives us nothing but the possibility of experiencing sensation; it is what we make of sensory experiences that gives us direct access to objects independent of our perceiving and conceiving them.

In being related to spiritual ends, our actions acquire a meaning which transcends the merely physical. The meaning conferred on things enables us to ascertain the **value** they have for us. Thus, we can do things casually to external objects without consideration of their meaning. Unless there is thought behind our actions they may be meaningless. Of course, there is always the possibility of finding reasons for whatever we do. Hence even a hypnotised subject will find reasons for the meaningless acts induced under hypnosis.

On the other hand, that which can be physically measured or categorised with any accuracy has no value apart from the act of being measured or categorised. Thus, for example, the physical sciences have no added value in themselves except in so far as we make use of them in fulfilment of our ends and purposes. Their meaning resides in the thoughts that we have concerning them and in the interest we show in them. Their use consists in what is done with them for some purpose or other.

We therefore give value and meaning to everything by what we do purposefully to them and by judging them in terms of universal notions such as truth, beauty, and justice. Whatever we do or think about with a specific goal in mind, has a significance beyond any physical or mental acts. This is because of the reasons associated with that goal and because these reasons must incorporate universal notions in their formulation. In deciding to step outside, it cannot be said to be a conscious decision to do so unless the person has formulated reasons for doing so and considered these reasons to be good, fair, pleasing or perhaps to be bad, perverse, or displeasing in the case of malicious motivations.

Thus, a teleological view of the notions of value and meaning is being taken here rather than a strictly conceptual or analytical view. This means that they are being dealt with at their most elementary level of immediate usage. The reasons for doing anything are more important here rather than an analysis of the words and terms being used in this description. Such an analysis is usually undertaken in the expectation of achieving objectivity and of eliminating the subjective or personal element.

In so far as the act of valuing is objective, it involves measurement which is only objective in so far as it uses generally accepted standards of measuring, for example, the thermometer. The value arrived at by such measuring may be objective. But the act of valuing in general is a subjective act where there is no objective standard of measurement by which an independent value can be ascertained.

Treating the notion of value as something objective has therefore led philosophers and economists into endless confusions and contradictions concerning its meaning and use. Not surprisingly, the term is thought to be 'ambiguous' and 'confused' in its use according to Najder:

> Both in everyday speech and in philosophical literature 'value' appears in three basic senses, which often overlap and are even more often confused.
>
> (1) Value is what a thing is worth; something translatable into or expressible by some units of measurement or comparison, frequently definable numerically.
>
> (2) Value is a valuable (a) thing or (b) property (quality); something to which valuableness is ascribed.
>
> (3) Value is an idea which makes us consider given objects, qualities, or events as valuable.[8]

This view of value is unnecessarily complex and unwieldy and is objectionable for the following reasons:

• Emphasising the worth and measurability of value means treating **the value** as objective and overlooking the subjectivity of the act of valuing where no measurement is involved. It means taking the act of valuing from the context in which it takes place, intuitively and directly, within our thinking about things and their value to us

• The simple act of valuing something does not necessarily involve measurement which usually requires additional acts of fixing criteria of measurement and so on. Valuing itself is a more simple and fundamental process which may involve additional acts such as measuring where objectivity is possible.

• Treating value as a thing, property, or idea objectifies it by detaching it from objects instead of regarding it as an interactive

---

8   Z. Najder, *Values and Explanations*, Oxford: Clarendon Press, 1975, p.43.

process linking the objects to ourselves. Things are valuable because we decide within ourselves to attach value to them.

Valuing anything, in the first instance, is a simple process of relating it to ourselves in some specific way which is only elaborated upon by subsequent acts of measurement, comparison, and judgment. Valuing at this level is holistic and involves the whole personality as, for example, in the aesthetic value which we put on works of art by our intuitive appreciation of them.

Dealing with valuing at this simple level enables us to link it with the process of conferring meaning on things according to the goals and ends we set ourselves. **Valuing**, in the first instance, is thus distinct from **evaluating**. Only the latter involves the measuring, comparing, and judging. To place a specific value on something is thus the result of having evaluated it in some way. The reductionist aspect enters into the picture here since the evaluation reduces the object to something else in the process. This evaluating in relation to universal notions is dealt with in more depth in Chapters Five and Six.

The same kind of account is applicable to meaning which can be conceived of, in the first instance, as the simple expression of what is before us whether in thought, perception, conception, judgment, or evaluation. The act of conferring meaning on an object, such as a pen, consists in putting into words what is thought, being perceived or conceived, concerning that pen. It is a meaningless object in the hand if I am not aware of its being there or have no idea what I am holding in my hand.

It is a prerequisite to reasoning in that finding meaning in anything enables us subsequently to formulate reasons and evidence for postulating its existence and its relationship to other things. Thus, reasoning is to meaning what evaluating is to valuing i.e. an elaboration of what is given the act of conferring meaning on something. Thus, to understand why one has found meaning in something and what that meaning consists of, requires the application of reason or judgment on that which is intuitively thought to be meaningful. We intuitively believe everything to have meaning and value before we have formulated our reasons for so believing.

It is in this respect that the holistic and reductionist aspects of our thinking meet with their reconciliation. The intuitive aspect of knowing that something has meaning and value and of formulating reasons for so believing, involves the holistic aspect. But the subsequent examination of our reasons in terms of evaluation, judgment, or measurement, is a reductionist exercise.

At this point this account of how we think converges with the usual logical, scientific or psychological accounts of what we do in evaluating, judging or measuring. What is different about this account is the fact that the holistic aspect is being brought to the fore instead of being ignored or treated as nonexistent. It is important to bring it to the fore because, as pointed out in the last chapter, that aspect embodies what is subjective about our thinking - the goal-seeking intentionality which brings us into touch with our environment and universe as a whole.

Value and meaning are intimately related in so far as anything of value must also be meaningful, and anything with meaning must be of value to the extent that it is meaningful. Both of them can achieve priority in different circumstances. Value requires prior expression when we are most personally involved, as in the case of aesthetic experiences. Meaning gains priority where the nature and content of what is valued need to be expressed. The chicken-or-egg paradox arises because it is uncertain as to whether valuing precedes meaning or *vice versa*. But this is only to note that they develop in conjunction with the acquisition of language ability which itself proceeds by trial and error as the individual relates sensory experience to the external reality with which he is confronted and as he learns to perform accurate acts of perception and conception concerning the content of that reality.

Value is given to things by us in relating them to a subjective core of preconceived values, whereas meaning involves giving expression to the conceptual content of the thing being referred to. Thus, in this view, the value of anything is sought beyond it, and its meaning within it. Both value and meaning come from making use of things i.e. by relating to them in some way. They are the product of referring to things but involve making an account of these things which reveals the nature of their relationship to us.

The criteria for judging the value and meaning of subjective accounts are **noospheric**. That which is generally valued and generally considered meaningful has its value and meaning in the noosphere of communicated thoughts and words. This is the proper place for ethical conclusions to be arrived at. For it is only within the noosphere that meanings and values can be fixed sufficiently for individuals to hold them in common with each other. Otherwise, everyone would have their own ideas concerning what constitutes these meanings and values.

Wittgenstein referred to this fixing of ideas as taking place in the language games and in the forms of life within which language activity takes place.[9] Such games and forms of life are only parts of the complex noospheric activity which includes all communicable thought such as the Internet and the

---

[9]   L. Wittgenstein, *Philosophical Investigations*, trans. G.E.M. Anscomb, 1953 - Oxford: Blackwell, 1968, p.12, §23.

scientific exchange of ideas and information. They are not ends in themselves but belong to the pluralistic content of the noosphere without which they cannot take place. This is only to say that it is in an overall social context that games and forms of life function meaningfully. This accords with what Wittgenstein when he says that agreement in the language used means agreement in the forms of life rather than in opinions arrived at.[10]

But the **reality** of the values and meanings which are conferred on things lies in what is achieved by making use of these assessments of value and meaning. What is achieved is not only practical and pragmatic but also aesthetic and sentimental. Even aesthetic experiences are real enough for those undergoing them. They are life-enhancing and worthwhile in themselves, even though they may be lacking in objectivity and factuality, as in the case of poetry and music.

The values that human beings bring into being through their goal-seeking activities, are both positive and negative. The positive ones are constructive, passive and relatively harmless in their effects on ourselves and our environment. They include the quest for beauty, symmetry, simplicity, and other artistic aims, as well as material accomplishments such as buildings, factories, institutions, and other artefacts of human culture. The negative values are those that are destructive, disorganised, disruptive, degrading, dismal, contaminating, and anti-social. Judging between values and deciding whether they are or not positive or negative is of course not always straightforward and simple. Learning to judge between them is one of the most important undertakings in a person's life since it is essential to the cultivation of mature and wordly judgment i.e. noospheric judgment which encompasses all human activity.

Furthermore, value of any kind has both a quantity and a quality. The quantitative value of anything is numerical in terms of its contents and parts, and of its external or economic value. The quantity of any evaluation may be numerically discrete or dense, according to how the components are separated from each other or the density with which they are or are not packed together.

The quality of value concerns the reciprocal relationships with which the thing valued has or has not with other things which are the same or different from it. The greater the number of interrelationships, the more the thing is valued qualitatively. For example, the qualitative value of a stone increases in being made use of for some purpose or other by a living being. It then relates to the latter which reciprocally relates to it. On the other hand, its quantitative

---

[10] *Op. cit.*, p.88, §241.

value is confined to its weight, density, chemical content, number of molecules, its buying or selling price, and other measurable properties.

Thus, the value and meaning which we introduce in pursuit of our aims and goals is here treated at the very basic level of our direct relationship to external reality and its contents. As value and meaning become more noospheric, and hence involved in our social communication, so they increase in complexity and generality. They become related to universal notions, and it is in this way that we relate ourselves to the universe through the increased understanding which universal notions make available to us.

4 Using Universal Notions to Achieve our Ends

> Since nothing in nature is exclusively final, rationality is always means as well as end. The doctrine of the universality and necessity of rational ends can be validated only when those in whom the good is actualised employ it as a means to modify conditions so that others may also participate in it, and its universality exist in the course of affairs. . . The ulterior problem of thought is to make thought prevail in experience, not just the results of thought by imposing them upon others, but the active process of thinking.   John Dewey[11]

In expressing our reasons for setting ourselves ends and goals, we inevitably use universal terms which apply very widely but have no physical existence in themselves. A creature that experiences hunger and sets itself the goal of easing that hunger, has an intentional object which is universally experienced by living beings. We call this by the universal term of hunger because we all know within ourselves what it is to feel a lack of sustenance, however differently that feeling may be experienced by each creature. By the use of such terms we are at one not only with other sentient beings but also with the universe which makes such unifying processes possible. This unifying universal theme forms the heart of the science of the human spirit because it makes us an inextricable part of the workings of the universe, and not just a random product of these workings.

The values and meanings that we introduce in pursuing our ends and goals, are important additions to the content of the universe because they make sense not only of our own lives but also of the objects to which we attach value and meaning. We use universal notions as go-betweens to link

---

[11] John Dewey, *Experience and Nature*, 1929 - New York: Dover Publications, 1958, p.120.

ourselves and our ends and goals to, on the one hand, our physical environment and, on the other hand, other people. The ends and goals provide the reasons for making such links, and the values and meanings constitute the adhesive by which the links are securely attached to each side of the divide. For example, a quest for beauty leads the artist to formulate the standards he is aiming for i.e. his ends and goals, and the value and meaning that he finds in the objects of beauty concretes his commitment to that quest.

An end is what we do things for, so that its formulation is always directed towards the future. It enables us to put future events in some order within our own thinking and planning ahead. Consciousness results from being able to relate to our ends so that we feel that we know what we are doing in our minds at the precise moment we are doing it. It is again a turning in of mental processes towards that unified self which is always striven for but which is ultimately evanescent and illusive. We are forever attempting to establish what our true ends are, but it is humanly impossible to grasp them all at once through a conscious act of will. But in our constant attempts to be clear in our minds as to what our ultimate ends are, we are exercising the human spirit within us to the best effect, however inadequate our efforts may prove to be.

What subjective about our inner experiences has also to be distinguished from what is merely physical. Pains which are physically caused are not intentional and not a part of the human spirit, for they are experienced by us as sensations directly impinged from without. Objects of sensory perception are similarly unintentional in so far as they are the direct result of our perceptual organs responding to external stimuli.

Thus, universal notions are used by us to relate our inner subjective feelings to the external world in which we find ourselves. Instead of our thoughts being narrowly related to these feelings in isolation from everything else occurring the universe, they are progressively expanded to comprehend the universe at large. Universal notions have a very general application and therefore have an added evaluative significance in achieving our goals. These include such notions as good, beauty, justice as well as all-encompassing ones such as the universe, society, and the human race. Their very generality contributes to their evaluative significance since they bring us into touch with everything 'out there'. Their use helps us to add value to the universe because we judge the importance or lack of importance of our actions in relation to them. As a result, our actions are more directed and purposeful in their ordering, simplifying, and beautifying the universe we inhabit. The processes by which this is accomplished are now to be discussed.

5 The Evaluation
of Life and Living

> Science is nothing but trained and organised common sense,
> differing from the latter only as a veteran may differ from a raw
> recruit: and its methods differ from those of common sense only as
> far as the guardman's cut and thrust differ from the manner in which
> a savage wields his club. . . . The man of science, in fact, simply
> uses with scrupulous exactness the methods which we all, habitually
> and at every moment, use carelessly.   T. H. Huxley.[1]

1 The Common Sense Limitations to Universal Notions

Universal notions such as: **the universe, the human race, the world, life,
society, good, beauty, justice, rights, truth, honour, honesty, grace, love**
and **affection,** may be called 'common sense notions' in so far as they are
held in common by everyone and are found in every language. These notions
have been imbedded in the common language of human beings, presumably
ever since language ability was first developed many tens of thousands of
years ago. They are commonsensical in that their meanings are very
commonly understood and immediately evident to every language user.
Indeed, the general acceptance of these notions contrasts with the lack of
general acceptance of religious beliefs among humankind. This suggests that
these notions are better equipped for forming the basis for a generally
accepted science of the human spirit than religious beliefs as such.

However, these notions are often applied beyond their common sense
usage according to people's personal aims and goals. They thus have a great
potential for good or bad and sometimes both. In so far as these notions
remain within common sense usage, they are static and dependable. But
because they are open to individual use and interpretation, they are also
primarily cultural and flexible conceptions which call for constant
redefinition, alteration, and elaboration, by succeeding generations in

---

[1] T.H. Huxley, *Collected Essays*, Vol. III, p.38.

response to the changed circumstances of society and the human race as a whole. This subversive aspect of universal notions is tapped to unleash the dynamism and the innovative powers of our culture. Therefore, this aspect must also be disciplined and open to constant scrutiny and criticism to ensure that the bad or harmful consequences of such innovations are minimised. For even our most benign and best-intentioned acts may have bad and unforeseen consequences. One example might be the bestowing of charity which leads people to become dependent on it instead of learning to fend for themselves. But the use of such notions in noospheric circumstances provides the discipline and restraint which they require.

The common sense deployment of these notions is necessary for the maintenance of the status quo and to ensure the stability of society and its institutions. They are constantly used in conversations, dialogues, debates, essays, and articles in which there is a noospheric exchange of ideas and opinions. When they are discussed and examined openly in the noosphere of the public arena, their extraordinary propensities are kept within rational bounds. But when these notions are developed in an *a priori*, individualistic, eccentric, cliquish or exclusive manner which is divorced from noospheric intercourse, their potential for good or bad remains hidden and uncertain. In being brought into the noosphere of dialogue and debate their potential, either for benefiting society or for threatening it, becomes more apparent. Without the external vigilance of noospheric scrutiny and criticism, the dogmatic and rigid use of these notions will continue unchallenged and unabated.

Within the noosphere, the universal notions are used holistically in pursuance of our ends and goals. That is to say, they are used directly and without undue scrutiny or analysis. But when their unexamined use leads to problems and misunderstandings, then it is necessary to reach a better understanding of them by reaching agreement or disagreement with others about what they are or are not. They are then reduced to their components and perhaps rethought on a different basis. For instance, concerning the notion of **life**, problems may arise as to whether it is humane, on the one hand, to prolong life unnecessarily in the face of unbearable suffering or, on the other hand, to take away the life of a unborn child which is merely unwanted.

Universal notions are thus processes **in** our culture rather than products **of** our culture. What they lead to is more important than what they are thought to be at any moment in time. We are to think about them only in so far as they may be clarified for practical purposes. To clarify them absolutely for their own sake is to lapse into dogmatic thinking concerning them.

The dogmatic use of universal notions finds its origin in the Platonic theory of forms which treats them as objects having an existence independent of any human being thinking of them. Contrary to this Platonic view, these notions are not identifiable things that may be defined and delineated in a coherent manner. They have only **contexts** in which they are used, and in relation to which they gain an intuitively grasped meaning. They have no lasting boundaries between their synthetic and analytic aspects. Their reality consists in their being more general and inclusive than anything they refer to. The more general those conceptions are, the more potential they have for changing their meaning and for being newly applied in different contexts. The fact that they are more general means that they are also more indefinite and flexible and all-inclusive as a consequence.

It follows that to avoid dogmatism[2] and narrow-minded thinking, the fluidity and indefinite nature of universal notions has to be stressed rather than their ability to be analysed and accounted for in any definitive or concrete manner. This means revising and updating Platonism by treating universal notions as highly flexible in their use by the individual. Any objectivity on their part resides not in 'reality' but their being brought out of the darkness of dogmatic subjectivity to bask in the sunshine of noospheric activity. They are thereby discussed with others and become the focus of group and communal activity instead of being defined, once and for all, by some isolated individual.

Having no essences means that universals are not particular things. They are instruments of evaluation by which we relate to external reality but not at the same time to any particular physical thing within that reality. They are the means by which we may evaluate our actions and attitudes in respect of what we are or are not to do in the real world.

The noological view differs from Platonism in that (1) the latter's high ideals are unexceptionable and ultimately unsustainable and unattainable, and (2) notions in the former view are treated as **working principles** which do admit of exception, are refutable and disposable, and are also under constant review and revision. Universal notions are therefore **hypothetical** rather than ideal. They are not to be treated as objects in their own right but only as the objects of constant exercise by the faculties of reason and judgment. We are never to cease using these faculties to bring these conceptions before the mind and to make sense of them anew. Above all, we are to constantly hone and reshape our understanding of these notions in relation to other people's views

---

[2] As defined in Chapter Two, Section II.

of them. In a spirit of flexible and adaptative thinking, those views are to be welcomed that challenge and even contradict our own because only in that way do we keep a fluid and open view of them.

2 The Teleological Deployment of Universal Notions

> I go among the fields and catch a glimpse of a stoat or a fieldmouse peeping out of the withered grass -The creature hath a purpose and its eyes are bright with it - I go amongst the buildings of a city and I see a man hurrying along - to what? The Creature has a purpose and his eyes are bright with it.   John Keats[3]

We deploy universal notions in fulfilling our goals and purposes when we use them to evaluate and to bring order and meaning into our lives. Their deployment in that respect goes beyond their common sense use when that deployment is personal and private to the individual whereas their common sense use is public and impersonal. The goals and purposes for which these notions are used may take them beyond common sense but they avoid eccentricity and dogmatism in so far as their use may be positively evaluated as, for example, good, simple, or beautiful.

The manner in which these notions begin to transcend their common sense foundation, and thus become a personal and subjective means of relating ourselves to the universal, holistic and all-embracing aspects of life and living, may be outlined as follows:

The universe is the most general and all-inclusive of all conceptions and is therefore also the most instable and indefinable of all conceptions. It is potentially so complex and unwieldy that it has a distinctive meaning in every context in which it is used because it will signify different things in every context in which it is used. It changes, for instance, with every new astronomical observation and every new theory concerning the way it originated or the way its processes may or may not work. The universe is not only the thing that has produced us, it also possesses us at a deeper level than we are yet capable of comprehending. But it is only at the personal and subjective level that its mysterious and mystical nature begins to arise, since it is impossible for any one individual to totally grasp its immensity and relate it meaningfully to their personal life.

---

[3]   *Letters of John Keats to his Family and Friends*, ed. Sidney Colvin. London: Macmillan, 1891, Letter to George and Georgina Keats, Friday, 19th March 1819, p.236.

The human race is not only the generic term for human beings as a group but also has important connotations for the noologist. This is because belonging to the human race is something over and above being a member of a group of all human beings. It enables us to bring the whole human race into our thinking as an entity worthy of attention in itself. But to have any lasting feeling of belonging to the human race, we must have a developed and mature view of the human race and its accomplishments, its failings, its merits and demerits. Thus, to have a secure feeling that we are fulfilling any kind of role in relation to the human race as a whole, we must have a subjectively developed notion of human race that transcends the common sense one of simply knowing that there is such a thing as the human race. It is therefore a prerequisite to feeling at one with the universe that we should have a notion of ourselves as belonging to and fulfilling a role *vis à vis* the human race.

The world is not just the planet, globe or geosphere which the human race happens to inhabit at this moment. It is something that belongs to each and everyone of us because we are living beings in the company of other living beings on this planet. We belong to the world because we inhabit it and it belongs to us because we can think of it in a positive way, as we think of our house, our business, our country, and our continent. We are thus responsible for it because it belongs to us whenever we contemplate it, in the same way that we are responsible for our arms and legs, and for our words and thoughts because they belong to us.

The notion of **the good** was perhaps the earliest judgmental notion arrived at by human beings. Learning to put a particular value on something in comparison with other things was one of the most significant steps taken by our ancestors. It enabled them to discriminate between objects in a rational way instead of responding mutely and instinctively to their presence. The subsequent development of such comparative and superlative adjectives as **better** and **best** seems to provide an impetus to the technological improvement that followed the advent of Cromagnon man. Where this development perhaps went wrong was when these notions were attributed by the Aryan peoples to individuals with the result that the notion of the aristocrat was arrived at. But when these words are confined to our ends and goals, they enable us to improve on things as opposed to valuing them in a passive way by thinking them merely 'good'. However, the chief good (*summum bonum*), being the best thing of all, is a Platonic notion that should never be decided by one or more persons for the whole human race. It is something that occurs to individuals in particular circumstances which will not be the same at different times or places.

Beauty is a notion that expresses our appreciation of what is given to us in life. There is little point in living unless we can appreciate the beautiful things that surround us in our everyday lives. But beauty is not only in the eye of the beholder as it is subject to noospheric influences. We often learn to appreciate what is beautiful because of fashionable influences, dominant opinions and trends set by artists, authors, poets and advertisers. In that case, we learn to see and feel the beauty that others have anticipated us in appreciating. Someone having distinctive taste can influence others into appreciating the standard of beauty and excellence laid down by that person. The notion of beauty is therefore as important from a noospheric point of view as from that of the individual experiencing personal, aesthetic feelings.

Justice is our way of making comparisons between things and events to arrive at supposedly objective standards of fair treatment for human beings and other living beings. In so far as such standards can be objective this can only be in relation to the noosphere of collective thinking between human beings. There has to be general agreement about what is just or unjust and this is arrived at by constant debate and discussion. A concrete concept of justice need not be aimed for since it makes sense only within the context of noospheric debate and not when it is confined solely to the thinking of one or a number of individuals. Even in noospheric debates on the subject of justice, it must never be forgotten that posterity is the ultimate arbiter of what is really and ultimately just, so that all judgments on that score are only provisional and never absolute.

Rights are due to all of us only in so far as we behave ourselves as human beings and are prepared to make a decent place for ourselves in human society. In so far as we claim any rights at all, we do so as an inextricable part of human society. Rights therefore come together with obligations and responsibilities. Without fulfilling some rational obligations and responsibilities, we cannot expect to retain any rights beyond those of being allowed to live an unmolested and solitary lifestyle. The measure of what are rational obligations and responsibilities lies in noospheric values. The notion of the noosphere in justifying the allocation of rights, also helps to reinforce and protect them. For the act of preventing any human being from exercising their rights diminishes the activity which comprises the noosphere. Such an act curtails their free and responsible contribution to the noosphere.

Truth is that which is discovered by the use of our faculties to establish what is really the case. But there are two aspects to truth which constantly vie with each other - that of correspondence and that of coherence. Seeking the truth involves both a direct corresponding with what exists in the world and an indirect accounting for that correspondence through an analysis of meanings. Truth in this materialist world has been too bound up with deductive logic with the result that its connection with such notions as honour, honesty and sincerity has been often overshadowed. It has therefore been confined to reasoning so that whatever makes sense in a deductive manner is considered to be truthful. But, as pointed out in Chapter Three, we are capable of inventing reasons for anything we do or think. Whatever you reason to be the case is the truth regardless of its correspondence to the real state of affairs or its coherence with the facts as a whole. Truth has to be tied to openness and to the honour, honesty and sincerity which flow from it if it is to remain above mere reasoning and be the arbiter of the correctness and justice of our reasonings. This is another function of the noosphere, namely, to provide the ambience in which such connections constantly reinforced so that our reasonings are scrutinised from all possible points of view and not allowed to hold sway in isolation from reality and the facts. The noosphere provides the connections which bring isolated individuals, groups, sects, cliques, companies, nations, and international organisations into the common forum within which all truths are ultimately decided in the light of history and posterity.

Honour is an expression of self-respect and self-esteem. We wish to behave honourably because our self-esteem depends on it. Generally speaking, people cannot live with themselves with any ease unless they know themselves to be behaving honourably. Taken to extremes, it means that the individual regards his honour as more important than any other consideration. This Platonic attitude manifested itself widely in the Middle Ages and was called 'chivalry'. A more enlightened view is that honourable behaviour is that which does not make us feel ashamed or ill-at-ease with oneselves. It is becoming behaviour that is worthy of ourselves. Thus, a dishonourable person knows no shame or guilt whatever they do or however they behave. It is not merely a matter of other people being ashamed or mortified by such a person's conduct. It is mostly a matter of the dishonourable person having lost that degree of sensitivity and self-awareness which allows them to be aware of the shamefulness of their conduct. Such a person has lost touch in themselves to some degree and no longer feels the effects of their behaviour either on themselves or on others. Thus, the notion of honour is useful noospherically because it enables us to call people's attention to their deficiencies in that regard and give them an opportunity at least to think about it and, if possible, do something about it.

Honesty is the best policy because honest behaviour contributes to one's honour and grace in the eyes of others. An honest person feels ashamed at any suggestion of insincerity and deviousness in their motives. They are justly proud of their disingenuousness which comes from being no more than they seem to be. Dishonest persons thus hide behind their outer appearance and know themselves to be different and more complex than they appear to be. They are untrustworthy because their ulterior motives get in the way of doing the straightforward and expected thing. Trust is the most important product of honesty without which society cannot function. Thus, from a noospheric point of view, the accusation of dishonesty is something that the individual themselves is supposed to take account of in their self-examination. Not to be able to take account of such an accusation is resonant of defects within a person's thinking about themselves. Therefore, punishment in matters of dishonesty is of no use unless it directly assists the individual in coming to terms with what they are and must do within a social setting.

Grace is basically what nowadays might be called 'style' or 'charisma'. A 'gracious' person has all the 'graces' which make for a 'graceful' person. A person having grace is a 'nice' person who enjoys being thought of as being nice. This notion has important consequences because it encourages people to be gracious and therefore be more sociable and pleasant than they might otherwise be inclined to be. It also helps people to reinforce their place in the universe and ensure that they feel at home in it rather than feeling out of place and ill at ease. Grace is that which is possessed by truly noble people. Thus, a large amount of graciousness in any society is supplied by persons who behave with nobility and honour. As Edmund Burke remarked in defending the rationale of the French nobility:

> Nobility is a graceful ornament to the civil order. It is the Corinthian capital of polished society.[4]

The form of nobility of course changes from one kind of society to another. The dominance of the primogenitary system in Europe virtually ended with the First World War. A new kind of **meritocratic** or **timocratic** nobility based on merit or celebrity, has been gradually coming to the fore ever since. But it all too often falls short of true nobility because of its lack of graciousness. An uncouth and uncultivated meritocracy does not amount to a nobility, nor does a timocracy which reveres people merely because they are

---

[4]   Edmund Burke, *Reflections on the Revolution in France*, 1790 - London: Penguin, 1976, p.245.

famous and well-known, regardless of their personal qualities. The importance of emphasising grace and nobility lies in the example which it provides of the proper behaviour for a human being to aspire to. Good manners, courtesy and etiquette are thereby brought to the fore.

Love is extremely important as an abstract notion because it signifies our knowledge of the depth of our relationships with each other. No other animal knows that it loves another in the sense of knowing what its feelings are. But it is all too easily confounded with physical attraction, desire, and lust. Love, in its best sense, is affection which has deepened into something more lasting and permanent because it is associated with specific relationships between those loved. In this sense, saying 'I love you' is an expression of a commitment to the person loved and not just an expression of unadulterated feeling.

Affection is, from a noospheric point of view, a more important notion than love. This is because it can be easily distinguished from physical love or sexuality. The affection that one human being has for another need not be tainted with sexual or physical attraction. To have affection for a person is not to lust after them but be concerned about them as a human being. To treat a person as a sex object is not to display affection for them but to treat them an object of one of our lowest and most irrational emotions. Focusing on 'affection' rather than on the more general term 'love' is deliberate because the latter is all too often bound up with sexual impulses. For example, 'falling in love', as something that exceeds the bounds of mere affection, involves an expression of a person's sexuality. Thus, affection is a better and more rational basis for human relationships than love because it is not confused by association with sexual attractiveness or the lack of that attractiveness. It is therefore more conducive to the free and unsullied exchange of thoughts and ideas within the noosphere.

In the above outline, the universal notions are not so much analysed as elaborated in terms of what we are able to do with them in a noospheric context. In using them in that context, they enable us to evaluate our position so as to arrive at goals and ends appropriate to us both as individuals and as social beings. This method constitutes a theoretical explanation of the way that ethical judgments function in our society. It therefore offers a theoretical basis for a more scientific and generally accepted ethical system than has been possible hitherto. Whether this promise is borne out depends on this science of the human spirit being developed more thoroughly and systematically than is being attempted in this work at this time.

3 The Mystical Aspects of our Universal Notions

The empires of the future are empires of the mind.

Sir Winston Churchill.[5]

Plato never did explain satisfactorily where his 'forms' dwelt and how we come to partake of them. We presumably catch hold of them somehow, like catching birds in an aviary. However, according to this theory, universal notions may be said to exist potentially in the universe and to be brought into being by our thinking by means of them. The potential existence of these universal notions can only be in the chaos that lies ahead of us in time. As we move forward through time and into the future, we are constantly re-ordering ourselves in relation to our past physical and mental structure. This gives us the opportunity to reconstruct our thinking anew from the chaos into which we are passing.

According to this reasoning, our universal notions are assumed to lie dormant in the body of the universe but not as identifiable things. They are coalesced out of the chaos of the universe by our mental efforts in making sense of our environment, society, other people and ourselves. They occur to us all at once as simple and complete wholes which soon lose their pristine simplicity in being thought about and subjected to analysis and deduction.

Unity lies at the heart of the universe, and every discrete object in the universe is tending towards that unity because of the gravitational and other forces which ensure that its own inherent unity is retained. Each object turns into that unity and partakes of it. The more internally complex an object is, the more it is organising itself towards that unity at the heart of the universe. Thus, in our case, the universal notions are products of our internal organising of ourselves towards that unity.

The scintilla of truth in the Platonic view is that these notions must have come from somewhere and have had some kind of potential existence. Otherwise it is difficult to understand how they could have come into being at all. Just as the mighty oak finds its origin in the humble acorn, so there has to be something pre-existent and seed-like from which these notions emerge. They cannot have come out of nothing whatsoever. Or if they did, then their origin is even more mystical that we can possibly contemplate.

---

[5]   Winston Spencer Churchill, 'Speech at Harvard University', 6th Sep. 1943, in *Complete Speeches 1897-1963*, New York: Chelsea House Publishers, 1974, Vol. VII, 1943-49, p.6826.

This does not mean that we have no choice over these notions since each act of conceiving a notion is unique not only to each human being but also to each situation in which it is conceived. The possibilities are infinite so that there is potentially an infinite range of choice of notions.

The important process by which we may understand better the mystical emergence of universal notions is by means of a **palintropy** or turning in upon. They result from a turning in of consciousness to reach the universe as a whole through quantum processes. Thus, the explanation which noology offers is that these universal notions are dredged out of our chaotic unconscious which is linked palintropically with the chaos at the heart of the universe. A fuller explanation of this phenomenon is irrelevant to the central theme of this book and will be dealt with *in extenso* in another book on this subject.

Universal notions are therefore an important intermediary between the individual and the universe in which he finds himself. But the stage on which that interchange takes place is the noosphere of communicable thought. It is only through the deployment and development of the noosphere that the individual gains increasing access to the world and its opportunities, and the universe and its resources. The importance of the noosphere in these respects has next to be discussed.

6 The Use and Value of the Noosphere

> The world was made to be inhabited by beasts, but studied and
> contemplated by man.   Sir Thomas Browne (1643)[1]

1 The Noosphere as an Object of Study and Contemplation

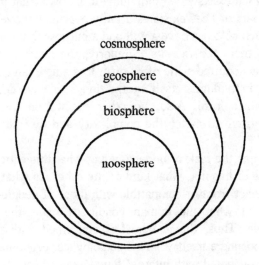

Figure Two: The Four Spheres of Evolution

The above distinctions suggest that the noosphere of communicable thought has grown out of the biosphere with the advent of sociable, language-using intelligent beings, just as the biosphere of living beings developed on the surface of the geosphere of water, rock, earth and air when reproductive organisms came into being, and just as the geosphere emerged from the dust and gas of the cosmosphere or universe at large.[2] These notional spheres are currently the preserve of researchers such as the following:

---

[1]   Sir Thomas Browne, *Religio Medici*, in *The Major Works*, London: Penguin, 1977, Part
I, §13, p.75.
[2]   Diagram is adapted from that given in P.C. Sylvester-Bradley's article, 'An Evolutionary

cosmosphere: astronomers, physicists, astrophysicists, and cosmologists.
geosphere: geologists, oceanographers, vulcanologists, and meteorologists.
biosphere: biologists, zoologists, botanists, and ornithologists.
noosphere: sociologists, economists, anthropologists, linguists, and noologists.

The nature of the noosphere itself is the proper object of study and contemplation for the noologist, in so far as he is concerned with understanding the spiritual aspects of the universe in relation to its physical aspects. The noosphere is the first entity we know of which is completely distinguishable from the physical universe as we know it. For it is a purely spiritual entity which exists as an individual in its own right in the same way that a colony of ants or bees exists as a unity over and above the individuals comprising it. Such colonies have a will and a purpose that transcend the will and purpose of their constituents. Similarly, the noosphere, as a unified cultural entity, has acquired a life of its own. It is a new kind of entity on this planet because it individuates itself by the things that we do, think and say collectively in our culture. Also, no other species on this planet has a communication system to match the complexity and diversity of noospheric activity.

The noologist has the task of understanding what this entity is, what kind of existence it has or has not, what kind of life it has, to what extent its ends and goals are distinct from or compatible with those of people in general and as individuals, and what the human conditions make the notion of the noosphere possible. Thus, the noologist is concerned with the nature and function of the noosphere itself whereas sociologists, economists, politicians, and the rest, are concerned with internal functioning of society and of human affairs within the noosphere.

The study of the noosphere is our key to understanding the needs of posterity and how best to contribute to posterity's well-being. For whatever contributes to the growth and development of the noosphere both consolidates it and points to its future. This applies as much to the everyday acts of so-called ordinary people as to those persons who have achieved celebrity status because current cultural values have given them prominence. Whether or not posterity will, in fact, agree with the latter assessment will be decided only in the future.

The notion of the noosphere is important because it unifies and provides a focal point for human intellectual activity. It enables us to rationalise the pluralistic activities of the human race without threatening or repressing them

Model for the Origin of Life', *Understanding the Earth*, Artemis Press, 1971, p.124.

or demanding conformity to preconceived norms. It constitutes a unity within which plurality can live and grow - *e pluribus unum* (one out of many). It is the kingdom of ends towards which all other human ends gravitate.

The noosphere is humanity's most important invention as its products could outlast us as a species and justify our having existed at all. Books, newspapers, films, discs, websites and broadcasts already document our noospheric activity. And only by our continued contributions to that activity do we justify our present existence. The single most important aspect of the existing noosphere is the present activity of people in communicating with each other. The physical objects produced thereby - the books, newspapers, films and other forms of recording - constitute useful by-products and proof of the existence of that activity. But these material records are not sufficient to be the noosphere itself. They are the tools and material on which we work in the course of making our noospheric contributions and are not ends in themselves.

Therefore, the noosphere is not an object of worship or idolatry since it is only there to be made use of as an artefact. We can no more make an idol of the noosphere than we can of the Internet, which is itself an intimate part of the noosphere. It is simply there to be used and made sense of, just like the Internet. It is to be enjoyed no more nor less than we enjoy a hobby or interest which involves us and gives added meaning to our lives.

2 The Origin and Use of the Noosphere

> Mankind, born on this planet and spread over its entire surface, coming gradually to form around its earthly matrix a single, major organic unity, enclosed upon itself; a single, hyper-complex, hyper-centred, hyper-conscious arch-molecule, co-extensive with the heavenly body on which it was born. Is not this what is happening at the present time — the closing of this spherical, thinking circuit?
>
> Teilhard de Chardin[3]

Teilhard de Chardin coined the term 'noosphere' meaning 'the terrestrial sphere of thinking substance'[4] which has grown out of the biosphere (or 'Gaia'). Taking this notion further than he did, we may say that the noosphere is the public sphere of thinking activity which has been brought into existence

---

[3] Pierre Teilhard de Chardin, *The Future of Man,* 1959 - London: Collins, 1969, p.120.

[4] *Op. cit.*, p.163. (It is pronounced 'no-osphere', not 'new-sphere'.)

by the language skills of human beings. Thus, the Internet, for instance, is a recent development within the noosphere.

He coined the term as early as 1925[5] and used it in some of his earliest published letters dating back at least to 1927. Thus, writing from China (Tientsin) in 22nd January 1927' he said: 'The "Noosphere" looms ever larger on my horizon. . . ' In a later letter of 27th Feb. 1927, he makes clear that the noosphere is for him one of the ways of promoting human unity and of overcoming the 'repulsion between men'; another way being the Christian faith. At this stage he appears to have thought of it as being the *Übermensch* which is to be reached in overcoming our emnities:

> It is really *the other*, the rival, whom we fear and hate in Man; and this aversion ceases as soon as we find a way to bring this other back into our unity. . . .
>
> It seems to me that this repulsion between men is something that must be overcome to arrive at a higher human state. To attain this result I have found no other method than to look at Man either impersonally, in the Noosphere, as a drop of water in the sea, or as an atom in Matter (why do you not love the Noosphere if you love the sea and the sky?), or else personally, in Him in whom, for the Christian faith, all are and shall be physically *one*.[6]

What has brought the noosphere into existence is the universality of language usage which has made it a viable and valuable addition to the contents of the universe. Because human beings are understood by each other to a greater or lesser degree (even when they speak different languages), their mutual

---

[5]   Cf. Julian Huxley's Introduction to *The Phenomenon of Man*, London: Collins, 1970, pp.13-14. In the *Encyclopædia Britannica*, (vol. 25, p.676), Vladimir I. Vernadsky is given priority in the use of this term, presumably in his book *The Biosphere* which was first published in Leningrad in 1926. But a recent abridged version of that book contains no mention of the noosphere. In Prof. Evgenii Shepelev's preface to that book, he states:

> In his last paper, written in 1944, he discussed the transition to a new geological era which he sometimes termed the *psychozoic era*. This was a new state of the biosphere termed the *noosphere* in which mankind as a whole would become a new and powerful geological entity able to transform the planet. (London: Synergetic Press Inc., 1986, pp.1-2).

Vernadsky may therefore have been responsible for linking the term with the biosphere but not for coining it.

[6]   Teilhard de Chardin, *Letters to Two Friends*, London: Collins, 1972, pp.56-7 & p.63.

comprehension is focused on this unified entity which exists as something beyond the material existence of human beings and contributes to their spiritual unity. The act of talking to each other brings people together within this common sphere because their sharing of thoughts is something additional to their physical existence in some sense. This communicative activity may be called noospheric as distinct from the physical activity of doing things in the world. Though the noosphere has no direct material existence, it is a product of the human spirit and of the subjective activity of all human beings who contribute to it as communicating individuals.

Thus, the notion takes account of the prominence given to language by philosophers of the twentieth century. At the same time, it helps to counter the disuniting effects of the resultant linguistic pluralism. As pointed out in Chapter Four, section three, Wittgenstein's 'language games' and 'forms of life' can be said to take place in this noosphere of continual intercommunication, so that the notion serves to unify the participants of different language games and forms of life. Such an addition to our thinking is required because the alienation, distrust and emnity, to which such pluralistic differences between people can give rise, may be overcome by thinking of them as taking place within a sphere common to all of us. Knowing that our different views, opinions, and lifestyles all contribute to the unified development of the noosphere makes such differences more understandable and therefore more tolerable. What unifies them under the mantle of the noosphere are the universal notions by which we co-ordinate our thinking and our judgments about things.

The intercommunicative aspect of the noosphere is the active part which consists of the day-to-day activity of people communicating with each other at every level. This active part interacts with its passive aspect which consists of the repository of books, tapes, films, discs and other recorded material that comprises what Popper calls 'the objective knowledge' of humankind.[7] The growth of the noosphere depends on the strength and intensity of the interaction between its passive and active aspects. This interaction manifests itself in the activities of education, research, the mass media, and all areas where knowledge is being used, and added to, for people's benefit.

The noosphere must not be viewed as a discrete, static thing as if it existed like a physical object. In its active aspect, it is a moving, shifting process in which we are all involved. As a passive receptacle of recorded human knowledge, it exists only as a generic term under which all such knowledge

---

[7] See the next section for more on Popper's view of 'objective knowledge' in relation to what he called 'World 3'.

may be classified, regardless of the physical means by which it is preserved.

The noosphere therefore exists as an abstract notion in the same sense that inflation is said to exist in an economy when prices rise. Just as inflation exists as part of a theory about how society works from an economic point of view, so the noosphere exists as part of a theory about how language and thought serve to unify the human race because of the common signs and meanings people are able to share.

Just as rising prices are evidence of the existence of inflation, so the Internet and other forms of intercommunication are evidence of the reality of the noosphere. The term refers to the phenomenon of increasing intercommunicability throughout the world. As a part of the noosphere, the internet signifies the ever-tightening technological unity of the human race by which people may regard themselves as a part of the human race as well as being parts of their community, organisations, and nation states.

The noosphere is the most fluid and flexible of all notions; its meaning is different for every person who contemplates its content. Because everyone's experience of the world is unique to themselves, their view of the noosphere is also unique to themselves. The meaning of the notion does not need to be fixed because it represents the very changeability of human thought and the fluidity of language usage by which that thought is expressed. At its apex, it is composed of general and evaluative notions such as good, better, best, justice, and beauty. These are also flexible and fluid notions but they are obviously more limited in their application than the noosphere. Everyone has their own conception of them in their private thinking about them. We establish common ground concerning them in our discussions and debates about them. Thus, in treating these notions as fleeting and transient we encourage constant discussion concerning their meaning and applicability. This in itself contributes to the growth and development of the noosphere.

The noosphere thus exists for us as an epiphenomenon of our culture. It is supervenient on the facts of our culture in the same way that the face on a portrait is seen as being an emergent part of the portrait. Just as the three dimensional appearance of the face is added by us to the two dimensional image of the painting, so the properties of the noosphere are added to our view of society by means of this theory which attempts to make sense of the noosphere and to show its potential usefulness.

In its cultural setting, the noosphere coalesces into lesser abstractions such as public opinion, the general will, fashions, cultural trends and crazes. All these changes in public opinion and culture are widely adopted through noospheric influences (through language and the mass media) but they may also be criticised, improved on, or cast aside. They have their place in the noosphere but the latter transcends and outlasts all such ephemera. Thus, the notion is needed because something remains while all human activities change and pass away. The noosphere endures even though everything else about the human race is in constant flux.

The noosphere provides a way of looking at the human condition and of making sense of it at a higher spiritual plane which is not so high as to be divine but which remains intimately connected with what people are doing and thinking in their everyday activities. It constantly develops and becomes spiritually more involved in relation to the increasing complexity of human relations. The notion of it therefore helps us to cope with the complexity of these relationships because it enables us to make sense of that complexity which otherwise seems chaotic and purposeless. The complexity is not chaotic in so far as it fulfils a purpose within the noosphere, that is to say, the purpose of contributing to its development.

Though it is a humanist notion, it is also transcendent without being transcendental. It is centred on the human being and is not beyond human values, considerations or aspirations but rather embodies them. It belongs to the thinking of every human being who contemplates it and has no transcendental existence outside that thinking. In so far as it does transcend the thinking of the individual, it is only to unify that person's thinking with those of other people. It remains within the bounds of human culture and society, just as our mental activity is confined to our brains and nervous systems.

There is no reason for us to regard it with awe and reverence. It is part of our thinking about things and belongs to each and everyone of us as a part of that thinking. We are to study and contemplate it as an object of our thought and not as something existing independent of all thought. Being only an artefact of human social activity, it has no significance whatsoever apart from that activity. It is important only in so far as it enables us to get things done and to make our appropriate mark on the universe as a species.

Its social importance lies in the fact that it brings us all together under its ægis. We have something in common with the whole human race because we are all participating to a greater or lesser extent in the noosphere and are contributing to its rational growth by means of whatever we do which makes sense noospherically. Even the law-abiding unemployed person may contribute to the rationality of the noosphere in giving the best possible example to others in the same plight. Just the act of talking to a stranger constitutes a positive contribution to the noosphere, however minor a contribution it may or may not be conceived to be. For even the most insignificant of contributions may have untold effects, such as changing the course of history, for all we know or can know.

The noosphere is therefore a repository of sympathetic thought in which we are able to see ourselves in the reflected thoughts of others. It is symbolic of the combined thoughtfulness of human beings in regard to each other. In fact, being thoughtful of others is what really qualifies us as welcome participants in the noosphere.

One might ask where do our philosophical debates take place but in the noosphere? Where are our notions of goodness and beauty but in the noosphere of communicable thought? Our immediate conception of them is personal to us but in making something of them by examining and accounting for them we must use words to do so and this immediately brings us into the noosphere, whether we think of ourselves as doing this or not. The noosphere therefore provides us with a place where Platonic notions may be said to 'exist' though not as being more 'real' than physical objects in the way Plato proposed. Their reality is confined entirely to their noospheric context which, as has been argued in Chapter Three above, is distinct from the context of physical objects.

There is therefore a range of 'realities' running from those of the noosphere to those of the physical universe and its contents. What is real depends on context and reference, and not on any objective criterion which can distinguish, once and for all, what is really real from what is not really real.

When we talk about 'living in the real world' we are usually referring to the reality which is encompassed in the noosphere. This is 'the real world' of economic restraints, social injustices, and environmental degradation. It is made possible because of noospheric connections and influences, that is to say, those that embrace the activities of the human race as a whole. These are judged to be 'real' from a noospheric point of view. But the real world of physics and astronomy concerns only the physical universe and its contents. In the last analysis, this real world is more basic and fundamental because a lack of knowledge of what transpires in this real world, leaves us open to arbitrary catastrophes from weather, earthquakes, volcanoes, asteroids, and meteors, any of which could threaten our very existence as a species. Nevertheless, our increasing knowledge of the reality of the physical world is itself a product of noospheric activity on the part of scientists. The scientific community and its activities are therefore a fundamental contribution to the noosphere without which its future cannot be guaranteed in the long run.

3 The Noosphere and its Past and Present Equivalents

A List of Equivalents to the Notion of Noosphere

(1) The 'Nous' of Anaxagoras
(2) The 'Logos' of Heraclitus
(3) The 'Tao' in the 'Chuang Tzu Book'.
(4) The 'God' of the Judaeo-Christian-Muslim tradition
(5) The 'Absolute Spirit' of Hegel
(6) The 'Society' of Thomas Carlyle
(7) The 'Moral Organism' of F.H. Bradley
(8) The 'Civilisation' of R.G. Collingwood
(9) The 'Three Worlds' of Karl Popper
(10) The 'Mindscape' of Rudy Rucker

The notion of the noosphere is perennial as it has recurred in many different forms over the centuries. Some of its equivalents include the following:

(1) Though the term 'noosphere' was invented by Teilhard de Chardin, it is based on the Greek word *nous*, meaning 'mind'. The word *nous* was first used in a metaphysical sense by the pre-Socratic philosopher, Anaxagoras (c.500BC to c.427BC). The term is used too indiscriminately in his philosophy to be considered a strict precursor to the noosphere. In his system of thought, the word virtually means God or prime mover:

> For it is the finest of all things and the purest, it has all knowledge about everything and the greatest power; and Mind controls all things, both great and small, that have soul. . . . And when Mind initiated motion, from all that moved Mind was separated, and as much as Mind moved was all divided off; and as things moved and were divided off, the rotation greatly increased the process of dividing.[8]

(2) Heraclitus's use of the term 'logos' is a more worthy precursor to the notion of the noosphere in so far as it is a unifying agent to which everything in rational discourse may be related. When Heraclitus said that 'everything comes about in accordance with the logos',[9] this may be taken as a unifying principle which means that every event may be described in words and hence

---

[8]   G.S. Kirk and J.E. Raven, *The Presocratic Philosophers*, Cambridge: CUP, 1969, p.375.

[9]   Cf. J. Barnes, *The Presocratic Philosophers*, London: Routledge, 1989, p.58.

brought into rational discourse that may be understood by everyone who is in tune with the conceptions underlying the words. Thus, although everything is in flux because things oppose each other endlessly, yet all this instability may be made sense of because of the logos.

(3) Another early precursor is the Chinese notion of 'The Tao'. This appears to fulfil the same kind of rationalising and unifying function as Heraclitus's 'logos'. But its use resembles the role that the noosphere plays in being 'above' us but not so far above us as to be worth deifying in any way.

> For it is by the Tao and the floating image of it that all creatures make perfect response to each other. Hence, what permeates all heaven and earth is power of personality, what is active in all creatures is the Tao. For the control of men from above is exercised through a round of duties, and the ability to discharge these with justice is an acquired skill. For skill goes along with a round of duties, these duties with justice, justice with spiritual power in a man, this spiritual power with the Tao, the Tao with Heaven.[10]

Nevertheless, the Tao is too all-inclusive and imprecise for our purposes. It introduces a measure of ethical compulsion because a man's actions in accordance with the Tao are said to be 'faultless' and 'perfect'. As it is used to regulate people's behaviour, it implies a measure of authoritarian compulsion which the notion of the noosphere need not include.

(4) The Judaeo-Christian-Muslim notion of God as the Supreme Being is similarly unsuitable for the purposes of this metaphysics. As is pointed out in greater detail in the Chapter Two of this book, this notion has being the source of more controversy and emnity than of enlightenment and mutual understanding. As everyone can arrive at their own views concerning the nature of God, the notion has more significance as a personal solace for those who are still fearful and child-like in the face of the unknown. In so far as we are prepared to take on a parental responsibility for what is happening on this planet, and ultimately in the universe, we have little need for this backward-looking notion.

(5) In modern times, the beginnings of the notion of the noosphere are traceable to Hegel's notion of the 'Absolute'. But the all-inclusiveness and imprecision of Hegel's notion, as in the case of the *nous* and the Tao, makes it unwieldy for our theoretical purposes. His term 'Absolute Spirit' perhaps comes closest to the notion of the noosphere in at least one passage of the

---

[10] 'Chuang Tzu Book', as translated by E.R. Hughes in *Chinese Philosophy in Classical Times*, London: Everyman, 1954, Part Five, Ch. XIV, pp.200-201.

Phenomenology of Spirit where he discusses it in relation to the community (die Gemeinde).[11] But the Absolute is being identified with 'spirit' or 'mind' and is too mixed up with the consciousness and personality of the individual to be useful in the limited, metaphysical context in which the noosphere functions. What is needed is a conception which points beyond the purely personal and subjective, but not so far as to leave the individual behind altogether, as God and the Absolute tend to do all too easily.

(6) Thomas Carlyle, admittedly under the influence of German idealists such as Hegel, used the term 'Society' to mean what is here meant by 'noosphere'. In the following passages from his brilliant essay, 'Characteristics', written in 1831, one may substitute 'Society' with 'the noosphere' with near perfect equivalence:

> To understand man, however, we must look beyond the individual man and his actions or interests, and view him in combination with his fellows. It is in Society that man first feels what he is; first becomes what he can be. In Society an altogether new set of spiritual activities are evolved in him, and the old immeasurably quickened and strengthened. Society is the genial element wherein his nature first lives and grows; the solitary man were but a small portion of himself, and must continue forever folded in, stunted and only half alive. . . .
>
> Man has joined himself with man; soul acts and reacts on soul; a mystic miraculous unfathomable Union establishes itself; Life, in all its elements, has become intensated, consecrated. The lightning-spark of Thought, generated, or say rather heaven-kindled, in the solitary mind, awakens its express likeness in another mind, in a thousand other minds, and all blaze-up together in combined fire; reverberated from mind to mind, fed also with fresh fuel in each, it acquires incalculable new light as Thought, incalculable new heat as converted into Action. . . .
>
> Such is Society, the vital articulation of many individuals into a new collective individual: greatly the most important of man's attainments on this earth; that in which, and by virtue of which, all his other attainments and attempts find their arena, and have their value. Considered well, Society is the standing wonder of our existence; a true region of the Supernatural; as it were, a second all-embracing Life, wherein our first individual Life becomes doubly and trebly alive, and whatever of Infinitude was in us bodies itself forth, and becomes visible and active.[12]

---

[11]   G.W.F. Hegel, *Phenomenology of Spirit*, trans. A.V. Miller - Oxford: Clarendon Press, 1979, VII, (C), p.463, para. 766.

[12]   Thomas Carlyle, 'Characteristics', in *Essays: Scottish and Other Miscellanies*, London:

It will be seen that many of the points made in this quotation are touched upon in this chapter in the developing the notion of the 'noosphere', albeit in less florid and enthusiastical language.

(7) F.H. Bradley, in his refinement of the Hegelian view, referred to a 'moral organism' which we must join as members if we are to realise ourselves as 'wholes'.[13] But this means losing our identities in the course of realising ourselves; a self-defeating procedure. Clearly, he views the 'moral organism' as something objective and therefore as relating to Hegel's view of the 'state'. But if we are to respect the individual's moral autonomy then the unifying agent must be viewed as subjective. It is something people do of their own freewill and not something that imposes its will on them. As noospheric activity is something belonging solely to the individual, this notion seems more appropriate in this context.

(8) R.G. Collingwood, in *The New Leviathan*, comes nearer to our requirements in that he views 'civilisation' itself as the 'mental process which goes on in a community'.[14] But he is concerned mainly with the contrast between barbarism and the civility which civilisation embodies. What he gives us here are the essential prerequisites to the development of noospheric activity. But he is not sufficiently concerned with what 'civilisation' means to each individual in working out their unique problems and aspirations as a part of 'civilisation'.

(9) Karl Popper's Three Worlds Theory (3WT) provides a metaphysical system whereby the workings of the noosphere can be amplified and better understood than otherwise. World 1 broadly refers to the material world; World 2 to the world of subjective experiences; and World 3 to the realm of objective, Platonic ideas. However, the theory is somewhat flawed in that Popper gives a different account of the contents of World 3 in each of the books in which he deals with this theory.

The notion of 'World 3' covers the objective aspect of the noosphere but it renders the contents of the noosphere inhuman because Popper's 'objective knowledge' is totally independent of human beings. We have already rejected such objectivity, especially in Chapter Three above, in favour of the view that objectivity results from human beings directly relating themselves to objects in conformity with their ends and purposes.

J.M. Dent, 1967, pp.194-196.

[13]   F.H. Bradley, *Ethical Studies*, 2nd ed., 1927 - Oxford University Press, 1962, Essay II 'Why Should I Be Moral?' pp.79-80.

[14]   R.G. Collingwood, *The New Leviathan*, 1942 - Revised edition, ed. D. Boucher - Oxford: the Clarendon Press, 1992, Ch. XXXVI, 36.1, p.299.

The 'World 3' notion can only be fully understood in relation to Worlds 1 and 2, with which it is said to interact in a complex manner. In conformity with his expressed aversion for 'methodical essentialism', he never did give one indepth, systematic, and coherent description of World 3, let alone of how it interacts with Worlds 1 and 2. And the latter introduce the intractable mind/body problem into the Three Worlds Theory. Moreover, his books fail to give us a consistent view of the 'World 3' notion, to say nothing of the 3WT.

In the book *Objective Knowledge*, Popper gives his first formulation of the 'World 3' notion where he says that it 'is the world of intelligibles, or *ideas in the objective sense*; it is the world of possible objects of thought; the world of theories in themselves, and their logical relations; of arguments in themselves; and of problem situations in themselves.'[15] He also says that 'human language ... belongs to all these worlds'.[16]

In the *Unended Quest*, he seems to refine and simplify the notion by making it comprise 'the world of statements in themselves'.[17] He is now apparently associating the notion with the world of logical discourse alone. The scene is now set to identify the contents of World 3 with the work of analytical philosophers in analysing and criticising arguments and contents with the help of logic.

However, in the more recent work *The Self and its Brain*, Popper restates anew his view of World 3 without referring to his previous accounts of it:

> By World 3, I mean the world of the products of the human mind, such as stories, explanatory myths, tools, scientific theories (whether true or false), scientific problems, social institutions, and works of art. World 3 objects are of our own making, although they are not always the result of planned production by individual men.[18]

In a diagram on a previous page,[19] he assigns the whole of human language to World 3. But the difference between this formulation and the previous one seems to be that he is thinking in terms of the *activity* of World 3 in the *Unended Quest*, whereas he is dealing only with the *products* of World 3 in

---

[15] K. Popper, *Objective Knowledge*, Oxford: OUP, 1972, p.154.
[16] Op. cit., p.157.
[17] K. Popper, *Unended Quest*, London: Fontana, 1976, p.181.
[18] K. Popper, *The Self and its Brain*, co-authored with J.C. Eccles, London: RKP, 1977, p.38.
[19] Op. cit., p.16.

the above account. He does not strive hard enough to reconcile these disparate formulations and fails to work out the notion of World 3 with metaphysical depth, consistency and clarity.

The Three Worlds Theory also fails because it runs headlong into the problem of distinguishing physical from mental events. In calling concrete, physical reality a 'world' like worlds two and three he seems to make it a function of the other two worlds instead of being brutally independent of anything we do or fail to do to it. Thus, we may ask to what extent can an unknown galaxy at other side of the universe be a part of W1 considering that it cannot form any real part of external world except in the imaginative W2 or the conceptual W3?

However, the 3WT may be clarified and made sense of in relation to the noosphere by representing these worlds as being three dimensional levels which interact with each other. This interpretation of Popper's theory has been put forward by E.P. Veening who portrays the three worlds as three distinct discs of equal area and importance.[20] Each set of discs represents the mental activity of one person. And the perception of an external object such as a building involves a link between three points: one on the world 1 disc, one on the world 2 disc, and one on the world 3 disc. Personal dialogue between two people involves an interaction between their world 2 discs, and a theoretical dialogue an interaction between their world 3 discs. The World 1 disc is here taken to refer to the facts about the material world, while the World 2 disc refers to the subjective values of the individual, and the World 3 disc concerns the conceptual activity by which both facts and values are rationalised in a social context.

Going beyond Veening's portrayal of this system, it may be further refined by making the three discs form a cone with world 3 towards the narrow apex, world 2 in the middle and world 1 forming the much wider base. In this way, noospheric activity in respect of each individual may be thought of as being directed towards the apex of the cone. The noosphere itself is then seen as being formed by the focussing of all world 3 apexes on one unified point. The noosphere is always beyond this point as something lying in front of the individual's thoughts and plans relating to the future.

(10) A more recent equivalent term to the noosphere is that of 'mindscape' which has been coined by Rudy Rucker in his book, *Infinity and the Mind.*[21]

---

[20]   E.P. Veening, 'Metalogue as a Key-Concept in the Methods of Philosophical Counseling' - a paper given at the First International Conference on Philosophical Counseling in Vancouver: 8th - 12th July 1994.

[21]   Rudy Rucker, *Infinity and the Mind: the Science and Philosophy of the Infinite*, London:

What he says about this notion opens up further avenues along which the notion of the noosphere may be developed. He says the following about it:

> All thoughts are already there in this multi-dimensional space, which we might as well call the Mindscape. Our bodies move about in the physical space called the Universe; our consciousnesses move about in the mental space called the Mindscape. Just as we all share the same Universe, we all share the same Mindscape.[22]
>
> It is certainly true that the Mindscape, for instance, does not exist as a single rational thought. For if the Mindscape is a One, then it is a member of itself, and thus can only be known through a flash of mystical vision. No rational thought is a member of itself, so no rational thought could tie the Mindscape into a One.[23]

But it is too much to hope that Rucker's use of his term should concur exactly with the use here being made of the noosphere. He says, for instance, that 'an idea is already in the Mindscape, whether or not someone is thinking it.'[24] This implies that the Mindscape is outside space and time, and then it becomes difficult to find a time and place for its use by human beings in everyday life. Nevertheless, the notion of mindscape may be said to relate to the noosphere in the same way that 'landscape' relates to the physical reality of a scene 'out there'. Thus, mindscape is the view of noospheric activity when it reflects upon itself, especially in purely mathematically and *a priori* terms. But the refinement and development of such a view is something for the future.

4 The Noosphere and the Good of Posterity

> Civilisation is not the servant of man. It is his master and tyrant; the superman that directs and enforces his actions to the greater glorification of Himself, and grants him the immense advantages of co-operation and specialisation only as a reward for abandoning his freedom of action to the higher aims of the communal spirit.[25]

Penguin, 1997, p.36f. Rucker also points out (on p.47) that Richard Dedekind, a colleague of Georg Cantor, coined in 1887 the word *Gedankenwelt* (thought-world) to serve the same purposes as 'mindscape'.

[22] *Op. cit.*, p.36.

[23] *Op. cit.*, p.48.

[24] *Op. cit.*, p.36.

[25] A. Raven, *Civilisation as Divine Superman*, London: Williams & Norgate 1932, p.40.

This pessimistic view of the development of civilisation implies that human beings will become enslaved and intimidated by this 'superman'. However, this is only an attitude of mind which could become a self-fulfilling prophecy. If we believe we are being enslaved and intimidated by civilisation then we become so. But the noosphere is not to be regarded as superior or intimidating. It is there to be used by human beings for their own personal purposes. It came into being because its existence suited and pleased people. So far from being a threat to their freewill, it provides greater choice and opportunities on which that freewill may be exercised. It has no power of command over human beings because its determinations depend on the actions of human beings and not vice versa. Nothing in the noosphere is predetermined as far as human beings concerned. Its future development is entirely shackled to the fate and activity of human beings. Thus, no matter how enslaving this notion of the noosphere might be conceived to be, its chief importance lies in its being a link between ourselves and posterity. For whatever is good for the noosphere is, by definition, good for posterity.

The noosphere, being nothing more than an abstract conception, could only threaten the freewill of intelligent beings if it is *thought* to be oppressive by individuals or if it is used by unscrupulous people to oppress others and to deprive them of their freedom. The very public nature of noospheric activities must therefore be a safeguard against either of these possibilities.

The future of the universe depends to a considerable extent on what happens in the present. It is not predetermined as far as the present events are concerned. It may be the case that, from the point of view of the universe as a whole, every event that is going to happen in the future has already happened. But here on earth we are not privileged with such a god-like view. For us, future events cannot be reliably anticipated or predicted at any particular moment in time. At each particular place in the universe these events are still in the process of being worked out as time moves on. The present moment in each place in the universe is a barrier which is only penetrated in the course of time. It is a barrier beyond which lies the great unknown. However, an understanding of how the past development of the noosphere relates to its possible future development appears to be one means by which the great unknown may be penetrated and ultimately conquered.

Firstly, the immediate future of the noosphere appears to lie in its further growth as the propagation of lifeforms occurs throughout the universe. This propagation is an inevitable and natural result of intelligent, language-using forms of life having come into being. The future of intelligent life in the universe seems to lie in the expansion and development of a noosphere of unified thought processes throughout the universe. This appears to be the way that life in general will be extended throughout the universe since intelligent beings will take other lifeforms with them in their voyages of colonisation. It is as natural for them to do this as it is natural for life of any kind to expand wherever and whenever it can, whether here on Earth or elsewhere in the universe.

Life strives to establish and spread itself in any environment which is remotely compatible to its subsistence. This is because each life form is fulfilling its internal purposes concerning its self-propagation and reproduction. But the fact that these purposes are thereby brought into existence, makes them important in relation to the universe as a whole. And the fact that an expansion of life occurs as a result of these purposes being fulfilled makes life even more imperative and important in relation to the universe as a whole. It is not just an insignificant growth of slime on a infinitesimally small and unimportant speck in the universe. It can be made sense of in relation to the universe as a whole.

This propagation is important because it means that life is thereby fulfilling its purposes in the universe by so doing. Life does not have a future in the universe in so far as it fails to fulfil such worthwhile purposes within the time allotted to its existence. A failure to realise the potentials inherent in all lifeforms means that they are failing to fulfil their purposes. For these purposes are obviously involve ensuring that life has a future in the universe.

Secondly, by studying how the noosphere develops culturally through the interaction between fact and value, we may get some indication of where the development is leading. For the accumulation of factual knowledge and personal experiences within the noosphere makes the understanding of the future consequences increasingly accessible.

What is factual and valuable about the activities of intelligent beings is important to the future of the universe because of their contributions to that future. In one respect, for instance, the personal experiences of intelligent beings may be imprinted on the fabric of the universe in a fundamental way, just as voices are recorded on tapes and discs. This recording of personal experiences may be occurring at the quantum wave/particle level of existence. It only remains for intelligent beings in the future to develop the technology required to tap into this source of information.

Thus, the continued accumulation of workable facts concerning the universe is necessary so that the goals of intelligent beings may be achieved. The accumulation of workable facts fulfils the spiritual as well as the material goals of intelligent beings. These spiritual goals consist in ensuring (1) that their lives are as valuable as possible in their effects and consequences and (2) that these lives have not been lived in vain. But these goals are constrained by the material limits of the scientific knowledge available to them. There are obvious limits to the extent to which they can ensure that the spiritual value of their lives is not lost but is preserved for an eternity.

Science therefore has both spiritual and material ends as far as intelligent beings are concerned. It has the spiritual end of producing knowledge which can be used to reveal the lives and experiences of living beings in the past. In that way the value of these lives is brought to the fore and no longer hidden in the mists of the past.

The future accessibility of valuable past experiences will help to justify the existence of the universe for an eternity. Such an accessibility will ensure that the universe has not existed for nothing. For all the experiences that have given value to the lives of intelligent beings will be accessible to future scrutiny. The aim is to ensure that nothing will be lost in the course of time. Thus, the universe's existence will be justified because the consequences of its existence will endure forever and will not be tied down by the passing of time.

Though the notion of God is to some extent a precursor to the noosphere, it is not helpful to equate the future development of the latter to the former. As is argued in Chapter Two, the notion of God has all kinds of anthropomorphic, paternalistic and mythical connotations that belong to past cultures of the human race and have no place in the future. Any advanced being in the future, which has inconceivable control over the universe, is no 'God' to intelligent beings. It is more like the 'child' than the 'father' to those intelligent beings who are mature enough to admit that there is no point in praying to and pleading with such a being. They cannot expect it to do anything for them since they are responsible for it i.e. for the prosperity of posterity, for which they may do their best if they want to do anything at all worthwhile with their lives. The importance of posterity in this scheme of things is now to be discussed.

7 The Presence of Posterity

Always behave as though you were being watched. He is a
prudent man who realises that he is being observed, or will be
observed. He knows that walls have ears and that evil deeds are
bursting to come out into the light of day. Even when he is alone he
behaves as though the eyes of the whole world were upon him, for he
realises that everything will eventually come to light: he regards
people who will later hear of his deeds as already witnesses of them.
The man who would like the whole world to see inside his home will
not be a prey to misgivings just because others can observe him from
theirs.   Baltasar Gracián.[1]

1 The Presence of Posterity *Now*

The notion of a God who is with us all the time and everywhere is better
understood as heralding the scarcely imaginable abilities of posterity to
reconstruct the past and to understand present events better than we do
ourselves who are living through them. Thus, noology looks forward to the
possible ability of posterity to have cognisance of our most initimate thoughts
and acts. 'Heaven' for a noologist is what posterity has in store for him in
making his life even more meaningful than it seems to be during his own
lifetime. Though a person's life might seem meaningless in present day terms,
it is perfectly possible that it will be much more meaningful to posterity in the
far future, assuming that intelligent life of some kind does survive into the far
future.

We may therefore assume that posterity is with us here and now in the
sense of their knowing what we are and what we are doing just as historians
know from diaries and journals who people were and what they were doing at
a certain time in the past. The presence of posterity is therefore not a physical,
or even a ghostly or supernatural, presence. Those who will compose
posterity are here with us only in that they will have access to knowledge

---

[1] *The Oracle: A Manual of the Art of Discretion*, (*Orácula manual y arte de prudentia*,
1647), translated by L.B. Walton, London: J. M. Dent, 1962, §297, pp.273-274.

119

about what we were doing at a certain point in their past. In that way they are able to reconstruct in visual form, by means of an advanced 'virtual reality', the scenes and events in which we ourselves are living our lives at this very moment. It is entirely possible that their technology will enable them to get inside our skins and feel and think what we are feeling and thinking, here and now. But they will only be doing so in the future and they cannot change events here and now. They will not have the ability to make us feel and think things or to influence us into doing anything other than what we are actually doing at the present time.

Thus, instead of being aware of the ubiquity of God, what we should consider possible is the ubiquitous vigilance of posterity. The idea of our acts being subject to perpetual surveillance has been recognised since the earliest times. For example, in the dialogue, *Phaedrus*, Socrates warns the lusty youth beside him that the cicadas in the surrounding trees are witnesses to whatever deeds they observe and that they report their findings directly to the Muses.[2] A consciousness of unknown and unseen witnesses to our most intimate acts has always been with us since the time we possessed the imagination to think of things not really being what they are immediately perceived to be. Thus, gods, spirits, demons, and angels were posited as possible witnesses of everything we do. Having a better developed scientific imagination than our ancestors, we can now assign this possibility to the future where the ability to reconstruct the past will be a distinct possibility, given the requisite theoretical knowledge and technological know-how.

The abilities of advanced beings in the future are only possibilities in the sense that the future is uncertain. We can be sure that if advanced beings are produced in the future then they will, sooner or later, acquire the abilities of ubiquitous vigilance. No one can possibly be sure that this will not be the case at sometime in the future.

The Great Day of Judgment (so feared by Calvinists) awaits us all in posterity wherein we will all be judged according to whatever we have or have not done in our lives. We may not be personally called before the tribunal of posterity to account for our failings, but our lives will be. In leaving these lives behind us to be judged by in the future, we can never be sure how they will be judged. All we can be sure of is that enough traces will be left behind of our having lived, and of how we lived, to enable these lives to be evaluated one way or another.

---

[2]   Plato, *Phaedrus*, London: Penguin, 1973, 259b, p.70.

Dying completely alone and unknown to the rest of humanity will not allow us to escape the tribunal of posterity, since everyone living and everything happening in the present will be known about in the future. Advanced beings in the future, by virtue of being more advanced, will have better technological means by which to study the past than archaeologists today have to examine the past of human beings. Being able to reconstruct everything which is happening in the present is only a technological problem of finding out how to do it. We lack such a technology now but our descendents in the distant future may well acquire it. If we takes our lives seriously then we must act on the assumption that they will do so.

But, as already suggested, these advanced beings are unlikely to have any more power to interfere with and change the lives of intelligent beings in the present than present-day archaeologists have with regard to past lives. This is not just because the freewill of intelligent beings is not to be interfered with, it is also because of the impossibility of reaching into the past to the extent of making physical changes there. The way that the universe is expanding into the future seems to preclude the possibility of reaching back into the past to alter it any physical way. Such beings will have greater power over the universe as a whole than over individual intelligent beings in the past. The possible abilities of intelligent beings like ourselves may only be actualised in the small scale, whereas these superior beings will only have power over large scale external events in the universe.

On the other hand, more advanced entities than intelligent beings would presumably be more spiritual than material, as anticipated in the form of 'angels' by scholastic philosophers such as Aquinas. This means that their lives would revolve round potentialities without the need to actualise them. Their existence would involve creating and destroying potentialities - a kind of all-encompassing 'virtual reality' or dream world. Their function in the universe might therefore be that of manipulating potentialities so that some are more available to be actualised than others. They might then be responsible for those coincidences and other events which seem to be more than just the product of random chance. If this is the case, then lucky and unlucky individuals are in the hands not of the gods but of these more advanced and wholly potential beings in the future. This kind of activity would not threaten the freewill of intelligent beings as it has no effect on their internal, mental activity; only on external events with which they are confronted. Thus, more advanced beings might have an influence over chaotic events, but not over the organised, complex decision-making of lesser beings such as ourselves.

Their ultimate goal would therefore be the perfecting of the universe by manipulating potentialities. This would mean creating a structure which is increasingly better at producing intelligent beings and at giving them a chance of a better and more fortunate life. However, this may not have relevance to the present universe; it may only apply to future universes which are spawned out of the present one.

If these beings do have any influence over present potentialities then there is a feedback operation involved here. It means that in benefiting posterity, intelligent beings are improving the ability of advanced beings to make more good luck and fortune available for intelligent beings in the present. In spite of the fact that good and bad luck have a random and ultimately unpredictable element because of the randomness of quantum wave/particle events, this does not necessarily preclude an element of good and bad luck which is 'caused' by events taking place in the distant future and by technological means beyond present conceptions.

This suggests that, in not doing his best to fulfil his potentialities, the intelligent being diminishes the future potentialities of the universe as a whole. His failure has a knock-on effect on his own life as it makes him less 'lucky'. His good luck is liable to run out since it relies on a conjunction of events that are outside his own control. But some of these events may be in the potential control of more advanced beings in the future. The welfare of these beings may depend on their lives being as productively beneficial to the universe as possible. The good things done in the life of an intelligent being will benefit these beings and give them greater potential to control the conjunction of events in his favour.

The ultimate destiny of the universe thus seems to lie in what it bequeaths to eternity to justify its existence. The fate of everything that happens in the universe depends on these events being an indelible part of eternity so that they might not have occurred in vain. Science in the far distant future may have the task of ensuring either that the universe continues indefinitely with its contents intact or that its contents are bequeathed to another universe spawning from it.

Whatever the reasons why intelligent beings are gaining such extensive knowledge and control of the universe, it is certain that there are reasons which are yet to be explicated and understood by them. If this were not the case then it must be asked how could such a possibility be even comprehended, let alone put into words which other intelligent beings can understand? The very possibility of gaining such understanding itself seems to be part of the fabric of the universe. It is there, in some sense, in order to be found. Thus, the aim of intelligent beings must be to strive for this better understanding of the universe and their part in it, if only because this task is there to be done.

2 Our Prospects for the Future

> Whatever may have been the original state of our species, it is of
> more importance to know the condition to which we ourselves
> should aspire, than that which our ancestors may be supposed to
> have left.   Adam Ferguson[3]

With regard to the future, the key questions to be addressed are:

Firstly, why is it that intelligent beings on Earth have acquired such an accurate understanding of the universe and of how it works at both the macroscopic and microscopic levels of existence? Was it entirely by chance that this knowledge has been stumbled upon? Or has it been acquired for a reason or purpose? Noology proceeds on the assumption that there may be indeed reasons why this knowledge has been acquired, and it explores the possibilities.

Secondly, it must be asked why each of us has values and experiences in life which are entirely unique to ourselves? Is this again purely a matter of chance or is there a reason or purpose behind it? If it is assumed that it has all happened by chance then there is no more to be said about it. It is only by assuming that reasons and purposes are involved that interesting answers are arrived at concerning the role of intelligent beings in the universe. And these answers need not be of the theological kind, since they are to be sought within our own understanding of the workings of the universe as given by the physical sciences.

From the purely materialistic point of view, we appear to have acquired all our abilities and the uniqueness of our experiences by pure chance. But this is a backward-looking, retrospective view that focuses on the past and reduces everything to its simplest and lowest common denominator (as is discussed in the next section). The forward-looking, prospective view reveals purpose and direction in the processes of the universe which appear to be occurring by chance when they are examined in isolation from complex entities that use these processes for such purposes as preserving their unity as an organised

---

[3] *An Essay on the History of Civil Society*, 1767 - Edinburgh University Press, 1978, Part I, sect. I, p.10.

whole. The preservation of the latter points forward to the future, and the fact that an entity will survive as a unity cannot be established beyond doubt by any physical examination in the present.

When intelligent beings have acquired the knowledge to enable them to exploit the resources of the universe, is it reasonable to suppose that they are not meant to exploit these resources for their own purposes? Is it not more reasonable that because these resources are there to be exploited therefore intelligent beings have every right so to do because they have the ability to do so? What other purpose could these resources serve except the purposes of intelligent beings? For intelligent beings appear to be the only entities in the universe that can even conceive of the possibility of exploiting these resources, and the only ones capable of formulating goals and ends for which these resources may be exploited. Therefore the ability to conceive and set goals seems to give them the **right** to exploit the universe as long as they are doing so for the best possible reasons they are capable of thinking of; that is to say, those reasons that concern the advancement of life in the universe and the securing of its future.

Even if these energy resources are strictly limited and are due to run out into the 'heat death' of the universe, this is due to occur billions of years ahead in the future. This gives intelligent beings such as ourselves time to get our act together. The fact of the matter is that we have all this time, together with the huge pool of energy, to fulfil our purposes and establish for ourselves why we are here. We are only finding the reason why as and when we acquire the knowledge and understanding to enable us to comprehend the workings of the universe. We have no choice but to use this pool of energy to gain more and more control over the universe for purposes which will become clearer as our scientific understanding of the universe increases.

Whatever design is discovered in the workings of the universe, these are purposes which we discover for ourselves in our own thinking about these workings. Such design does not presuppose the existence of any God or creator. It means only that the natural workings of the universe through time result from an interplay between chance events and determinable causes. Such a design in the universe would make increasing sense in the future, as its workings are better understood. But the more understanding we gain, the less room there is for any design independent of our thinking about the universe, as evolutionists such as Richard Dawkins are showing us.

Thus, the universe exists as something that is capable of being exploited by intelligent beings. So far from being worshipped or held in fear or awe because of its unthinkable hugeness, the universe is no more than the energy bread-basket of intelligent beings. Moreover, it is not worth deifying as it does nothing in itself. Only natural processes and entities **in** the universe achieve anything.

The real 'Anthropic Principle' is not that 'the universe must be such as to admit conscious beings in it at some stage',[4] but that intelligent beings have the opportunity to make of the universe what they will. The universe did not have to be the way it is, but now that it has actually produced intelligent beings, it is up to these beings to use that intelligence for the highest and best ends of which they are capable of thinking.

The fact that there are so many opportunities for intelligent beings to make something of the universe, in terms of the available energy and the unlimited space in which to expand *willy nilly,* seems to suggest that it is all there to be used for that specific purpose. But this is an illusion. As more facts are established about the universe, the more that intelligent beings will be able to do in the universe. They will be able to formulate more ambitious aims and goals concerning what they can accomplish in the universe. Thus, a better understanding of the universe leads to more value being put upon it and on what can be done in it. As a result, intelligent beings will have more reasons to believe that they have definite purposes to fulfil in the universe. The design of the universe will therefore be entirely of their own making.

Both the 'strong' and 'weak' anthropic principles result from retrospective views of the place of intelligent beings in the universe. They interpret facts about the past of the universe in terms of what has now been produced by the workings of the universe i.e. increasingly complex entities including intelligent beings. But the possibility cannot be excluded that, at certain points in time, the universe **could have been** different and therefore **might not have** produced intelligent beings at all. To rule out that possibility would be to assume that chance has not played a part in producing the universe as it is now. These anthropic principles are therefore too deterministic to fit the facts as they are. This includes the 'participatory anthropic principle' which assumes that 'observers are necessary to bring the universe into being'. But this cannot be known for certain without begging the question, namely, why do observers exist in the first place?

Even the 'final anthropic principle' takes too much for granted, that is to say, that 'intelligent information processing must come into existence in the

----

[4]   B. Carter, 'Large Number Coincidences and the Anthropic Principle in Cosmology', in *Confrontation of Cosmological Theories with Observation*, ed. M.S. Longair, Dordrecht: Reidel, 1974, p.291.

universe, and, once it comes into existence, it will never die out'.[5]   Just as evolutionary processes can regress and produce simpler rather than more complex forms, so it is conceivable that complex information patterns can be degraded and be lost to the universe. In so far as the information processing of intelligent beings is concerned, this will never die out only if these beings make the effort, from generation to generation, to ensure that that information is passed on and is not lost. However, human history indicates that civilisations come and go, and that much of their cultural products are lost as a consequence. Thus, the will to preserve cultural advances for posterity is all important.

Whereas Barrow and Tipler's book is admirable, Tipler's recent book, *The Physics of Immortality,* is a disappointing work considering that the author purports to be a respectable and reliable scientist. It has rightly been called 'a monumentally silly book' by a reviewer in the *Times Higher Educational Supplement.* Tipler starts off making assumptions which he acknowledges to be doubtful and speculative, and then proceeds to rely on them to reach apodictic and indisputable predictions concerning the way things will turn out to be in the far distant future. He does not begin to take account of the chaotic and unpredictable events in changing the way the future works out. How can he **know** for certain that life having come into existence will **never** die out? One can imagine events which would bring it completely to an end on this planet, and presumably on any other planet that happens to have life. Life is subject to the uncertainty of chaotic events and it will remain so until intelligent life achieves the power to secure its own future. In short, his arguments are thoroughly bogus from a common sense point of view, let alone a philosophical or a scientific one. Moreover, his picture of the future is that it will all come out right in the end, no matter what we do in the present. We are all scheduled to be resurrected at Omega Point and to live happier ever after. So why should we bother doing anything at all during our life times? It is all going to turn out for the best in the best of all possible futures, which is Panglossian nonsense. Tipler is not living in the real universe, the nature of which, let alone the future of which, we know to be ultimately beyond our capacities to fathom out completely.

---

[5]   J.D. Barrow & F. Tipler, *The Anthropic Cosmological Principle*, Oxford: OUP, 1988, p.23.

3 Noology as a Pointer towards Posterity

> He [the poet] must write as the interpreter of nature, and the
> legislator of mankind, and consider himself as presiding over the
> thoughts and manners of future generations; as a being superiour to
> time and place. Samuel Johnson[6]

The noological view is that the future is where all current problems facing life
and the human race may be solved. The best we can do in the present is to
ensure that there is a future for life and the human race on this planet and
elsewhere in the universe. This is a hard enough task in view of all the
problems we are creating because of our struggles to improve everyone's
standard of life. But we are at our best as creatures struggling against an
uncertain future.

If we can ensure a future for our descendents then all problems which
seem unsolvable at the moment have at least a possibility of being solved at
some time in the future. But this does not mean that all problems whatsoever
are to be left to future generations to be solved. A failure to do its best to cope
adequately with those problems which are within its power to solve, will
reflect badly on the honour and reputation of the present generation. It is thus
incumbent on that generation to justify its existence in terms of how its
actions and inactions will appear in the eyes of future generations. Not to do
so is to lack the sensitivity and foresight worthy of self-respecting human
beings.

The human race is special to the universe not because it holds a high
position in an evolutionary ladder but because of its future potential and its
ability to plan for the future and to foresee possibilities which will make for a
better future. But looking to the future with anything less than fear and
trepidation is a relatively recent occurrence in our civilisation. The human
race has not until this century looked forward to the future with a view to
planning its long term future. Before the 19th century, people habitually
looked to the past for inspiration. To them, the future seemed to promise
decline, disappointment, uncertainties, unforeseeable dangers and diseases. It
seemed to be destined to be worse than the past. And future generations were
not expected to do any better than past generations.

As late as 1852, Auguste Comte, the apostle of scientific positivism, was
writing that 'The living are always . . . more and more under the government
of the dead: such is the fundamental law of the human order.' By that he

---

[6] Samuel Johnson, *Rasselas*, 1759 - London: Penguin, 1986, ch. X, p.62.

meant that the present achievements of humankind are necessarily less and less important than past achievements so that the past will increasingly dominate the present. (Hence his worship of past heroes in his Church of Humanity, see the Introduction of this book) He was however saying this when 19th century technology was already changing the face of Western Europe to a greater extent than ever before, and Victorian heroes were accomplishing far more than their ancestors had dreamed of, for instance, in respect of their engineering achievements such as bridges, trains, ships, and factories.

With the publication of Darwin's *The Origin of Species* in 1859, with its idea of evolutionary change and development, the possibility of things being better in the future began to seem more realistic than before, as change and development were viewed as an objective and natural part of the world we live in. Thus, the writings of Herbert Spencer, for instance, explored the possibilities of things becoming more complex and developed in the future. This is because he defined evolution in terms of matter passing 'from an indefinite, incoherent homogeneity to a definite, coherent heterogeneity.'[7] Thus, things become more evolved in the future when they pass from a relatively simple state to a more internally organised state.

H.G. Wells assumed the mantle of an apostle of this new attitude when, in 1902, he delivered an important lecture at the Royal Institution entitled *The Discovery of the Future*. In this lecture, Wells distinguished two attitudes of mind:- the backward-looking 'legal mind' and the forward-looking 'creative mind'.

> The first of these two types of mind, and it is I think the predominant type, the type of the majority of living people, is that which seems scarcely to think of the future at all, which regards it as a sort of blank non-existence upon which the advancing present will presently write events. The second type, which is I think a more modern and much less abundant type of mind, thinks constantly and by preference of things to come, and of present things mainly in relation to the results that must arise from them. The former type of mind, when one gets it in its purity, is retrospective in habit, and it interprets the things of the present, and gives value to this and denies it to that, entirely in relation to the past. The latter type of mind is constructive in habit, it interprets the things of the present and gives value to this and that, entirely in relation to the things designed or foreseen. [8]

[7]   Herbert Spencer, *First Principles*, 1862 - London: Watts & Co., 1945, Ch.XVII, p.358.

[8]   *The Discovery of the Future*, ed. by P. Parrinder, London: PNL Press, 1989, p.19.

Wells acknowledged that these are two extreme attitudes of mind and that 'the great mass of people occupy an intermediate position between these extremes'.[9] But he argued that our civilisation is becoming increasingly oriented towards the future and towards coping with all the problems that our increasing complicated society is creating. Thus, it is necessary for the good of civilisation that people look as much to the future as to the past. The study of the future ought now to be pursued just as rigorously as the study of the past. 'The greatness of human destiny' lies in what we are about to make of it. That greatness does not lie in our feeble and uncoordinated actions in the past. It consists in what is to come and in our present efforts to ensure that things are better in the future. Everything in the past has been, as Wells said, 'but the twilight before the dawn' and everything accomplished by the human mind in the past has been 'but the dream before the awakening.'[10]

Nowadays, we are understandably less rosy and optimistic about the future prospects. It is now clear to us that the human race must always work very hard to ensure its place in the future, in view of its destruction of its environment and the endless possibility of catastrophes such as comets, volcanoes, diseases spoiling our promising future. Nevertheless, we have to believe in the future prospects of the human race before these prospects can be realised. And it is important to have a forward-looking view which, following Wells, we may call 'prospectivist' as opposed to the 'retrospectivist' or backward-looking view.

Thus, in believing in future possibilities, the noological view is **PROSPECTIVIST** as opposed to **RETROSPECTIVIST**. For the latter only looks to the past and anticipates the future only in terms of the past and its achievements and failures. Prospectivism is concerned with looking forward to the future and using the past for future purposes, rather than looking back to the past as an end in itself. Prospectivism aims to anticipate the consequences which changes bring about through time, and it uses an understanding of past events with a view of anticipating something different in the future. The strength of the prospectivist's vision is such that he sees the future as a place to be looked towards, whereas the retrospective thinker is too pre-occupied with the past to waste his time speculating about the future.

It is true, as Edmund Burke put it, that 'People will not look forward to posterity, who never look backward to their ancestors'.[11] But this backward-

---

[9] *Op. cit.*, p.20.

[10] *Op. cit.*, p.36. See page one of the Introduction of this book for the full quotation.

[11] Edmund Burke, *Reflections on the Revolution in France*, 1790 - London: Penguin, 1976, p.119.

looking is always from the perspective of a forward-looking attitude of mind. To be facing the past all the time and without treating the future as any different from the past, is what is here meant by 'retrospectivism'. The prospectivist thus looks back to the past to learn how to move forward to better things. He does not wish to keep the future changelessly in the image of the past as the retrospectivist does.

The retrospective view leads to reductionism in science and philosophy. It means, for instance, that the facts of nature are examined regardless of their application to an understanding of the future. Its procedure inevitably reduces everything to simpler elements and is typically the attitude of mind of the materialist scientist. However, scientists who understand the significance of 'the new physics' are less prone to this attitude of mind: see, for example, the books of popular science writers such as Paul Davies and Roger Penrose.

Prospectivism is therefore concerned with the opposite procedure, whereby things are built up through time into more complex entities. It examines the potentialities which are actualised by the activities of complex entities in the universe. This is an 'unnatural' aspect of the universe which retrospectivism overlooks because it concentrates purely on the 'natural' aspects of the universe. The latter are factual occurrences which determine the way things are, but only **retrospectively**.

Noology explores how the 'natural' workings of the universe produce 'unnatural' wonders which are new to it and may not be predicted from an examination of its pre-existing state. For example, the properties of helium, carbon, iron and other elements go beyond anything contained in the nuclear particles that compose them. Thus, living and intelligent beings are both 'natural' and 'unnatural' in the same way that the universe itself is. They bring novel and unique features into being through making their choices and having their experiences of life.

What is 'natural' about everything in the universe is usually deterministic, while the 'unnatural' aspect is the source of freewill. The latter makes the future uncertain for intelligent beings because of their ignorance of the full consequences of our choices. New and unexpected things are being brought into being because these consequences are 'unnatural' and hence undetermined and unpredictable. If we are to understand what the future has in store for intelligent beings then we want to know why and how these novelties are introduced into the universe. For **prospectivism** is concerned with how the unnatural features of the universe make differences and cause changes which accumulate into the complexities and varieties of things and events in the universe.

In the retrospective view, the future is expected either to be similar to the past, or to be worse than the past. There is nothing new under the sun and, if there is, then it cannot be for the better. The prospective view is not necessarily any more optimistic, but it takes a more realistic view of the capabilities of intelligent beings. It expects better things in the future only if these beings work hard enough and wisely enough to ensure that things are indeed better.

The prospective view takes account of the fact that entities are increasingly organising themselves so that they may better fulfil their purposes in the future. These purposes include the act of actualising their potentialities; an act which can never be detected in any analysis of presently occurring physical processes. The examination of the latter only reveals decaying, entropic processes which fulfil no purpose in themselves but only in the way they contribute to the complex whole to which they belong. And the purpose of the whole entity is only revealed in its potentialities which by definition belong to the future activity and have no physical existence in the present.

The prospectivist approach means consolidating the gains achieved by civilisation by showing how valuable these gains are from the point of view of posterity. These gains are to be cherished and constantly brought to mind so that their value is not forgotten. Only in that way are they preserved and made available for future generations. Seeing these gains as being an inextricable part of the noosphere is one way of ensuring this. Indeed, the ability to distinguish what are valuable additions to civilisation from those changes which are not valuable, depends on such a noospheric judgement. From that point of view, the changes may be judged to be either compatible or incompatible with the larger aims and objectives of the human race and of life in general. Those that are judged to be compatible, may be considered worthy gains achieved by civilisation.

Thus, the noological outlook itself provides a means of judging what is good or bad for civilisation from the long term point of view. The systematic development of this aspect of noology alone might contribute towards making the study of the future much more of a respected and informative science than it is at this time.

In conclusion, therefore, this proposed science of the human spirit is not a substitute for organised religion but an attempt to show the value and importance of the religious outlook from a scientific point of view. It perhaps suggests that such a substitute is both desirable and necessary. But the science of the human spirit is an attempted contribution to human knowledge and understanding and not a religion in itself. In the words of Francis Bacon: 'it is not an opinion to be held, but a work to be done'.[12]

---

[12]   See the quotation in Chapter One, section 3.

Bibliography
of Texts Cited

	Page Nos
Anscombe, G.E.M. (1957), *Intention,* Oxford: Blackwell	66
Armstrong, D.M. (1993), *A Materialist Theory of the Mind,* London: Routledge	61, 70
Armstrong, K. (1993), *A History of God,* London: Heineman	42, 43
Bacon, F. (1905), 'The Great Instauration' in *The Philosophical Works of Francis Bacon,* London	16
Bacon, F. (1620), *Novum Organum,* London: Book One	67
Barnes, J. (1989), *The Presocratic Philosophers,* London: Routledge	109
Barrow, J.D. & Tipler, F. (1988), *The Anthropic Cosmological Principle,* Oxford: OUP	126
Binning, H. (1840), *The Works of the Rev. Hugh Binning,* Edinburgh: William Whyte	30, 31
Bohm, D. (1981), *Wholeness and the Implicate Order,* London: RKP	77
Bonhoeffer, D. (1959), *Letters and Papers from Prison,* London: Fontana	42
Bradley, F.H. (1962), *Ethical Studies,* Oxford University Press	112
Browne, Sir T. (1977), *Religio Medici,* in *The Major Works,* London: Penguin	101
Buckle, H.T. (1906), *History of Civilisation in England,* London: Henry Frowde	30
Burke, E. (1976), *Reflections on the Revolution in France,* London: Penguin	96, 129
Carlyle, T. (1967), 'Characteristics', *Essays: Scottish and Other Miscellanies,* London: J.M. Dent	111
Carter, B. (1974), 'Large Number Coincidences and the Anthropic Principle in Cosmology', *Confrontation of Cosmological Theories with Observation,* ed. M.S. Longair, Dordrecht: Reidel	125
Churchill, W. S. (1974), 'Speech at Harvard University', 6th Sep. 1943, *Complete Speeches 1897-1963,* New York: Chelsea House	98

Page Nos

Cicero, *De Republica*   57

Collingwood, R.G. (1992), *The New Leviathan*, ed. D. Boucher,
    Oxford: the Clarendon Press   112

Copleston, F.C. (1962), *A History of Philosophy*, Image Books   9

Copleston, F.C. (1964), *The Existence of God*, ed. John Hick,
    London: Macmillan   9

Darwin, C. (1968), *Voyage of the Beagle*, London: Heron Books   34

Davidson, D. (1982), 'Mental Events', *Essays on Actions and
    Events*, Oxford: the Clarendon Press   68

Davies, P. (1995), *The Cosmic Blueprint*, London: Penguin   78

Descartes, R. (1986), *Meditations on First Philosophy*, Cambridge:
    CUP   53

Descartes, R. (1997), 'Rules for the Direction of the Mind' *Key
    Philosophical Writings*, Ross - Ware: Wordsworth   53

Dewey, J. (1958), *Experience and Nature*, New York: Dover
    Publications   86

Dostoyevsky, F. (1985), *The Brothers Karamazov*, London:
    Penguin   32

Farb, P. (1978), *Humankind*, St. Albans: Triad/Panther   39

Ferguson, A. (1978), *An Essay on the History of Civil Society*
    Edinburgh University Press   123

Fichte, J.G. (1982), *Wissenschaftlehre*, trans. by P. Heath & J.
    Lachs, Cambridge: CUP   16

Fowles, J. (1980), *The Aristos*, London: Triad/Granada   15

Gracián, B. (1962), *The Oracle: A Manual of the Art of Discretion*,
    trans. by L.B. Walton, London: J. M. Dent   119

Hegel, G.W.F. (1979), *Phenomenology of Spirit*, trans. A.V. Miller
    Oxford: Clarendon Press   111

Heidegger, M. (1987), *Being and Time*, Oxford: Blackwell   54

Hick, J. (1964), *The Existence of God*, London: Macmillan   9

Hofstadter, D. (1980), *Gödel, Escher, Bach: An Eternal Golden
    Braid*, London: Penguin   60

Hofstadter, D. (1982), *The Mind's I*, London: Penguin   56, 76

Hughes, E.R. (trans.), (1954), *Chinese Philosophy in Classical
    Times*, London: Everyman   110

Huizinga, J. (1970), *Homo Ludens*, London: Granada Publishing   28

Hume, D. (1978), *A Treatise of Human Nature* - ed. Nidditch,
    Oxford: the Clarendon Press   67

Hume, D. (1990), *Dialogues Concerning Natural Religion*,
    London: Penguin   38
Huxley J. (1970), Introduction to *The Phenomenon of Man*,
    London: Collins   104
Huxley, T.H. (1902), *Collected Essays*, Vol. III   89
Irwin, T. (1989), *Classical Thought*, Oxford: OUP   39
James, W. (1960), *Varieties of Religious Experience*, London:
    Collins   24
James, W. (1972), *Pragmatism and Other Essays*, New York:
    Washington Square Press   76
James, W. (1967) On a Certain Blindness in Human Beings',
    Selected Papers on Philosophy, London: Dent   52
Johnson, S. (1986), *Rasselas*, London: Penguin   127
Kant, I. (1964), *The Critique of Pure Reason*, trans. Kemp Smith,
    London: Macmillan,   16
Keats, J. (1891), *Letters of John Keats to his Family and Friends*,
    ed. Sidney Colvin, London: Macmillan   92
Kenny, A. (1992), *The Metaphysics of Mind*, Oxford: OUP   60
Kirk, G.S. and Raven, J.E. (1957), *The Presocratic Philosophers*
    Cambridge: CUP, 1969   109
Koestler, A. (1983), *Janus: A Summing Up*, London: Pan Books   75
Kripke, S. (1980), *Naming and Necessity*, Oxford: Blackwell   51
Kurtz, P. (1997), 'The Evolution of Humanism', *The New Humanist*,
    Vol. 112, no. 2   56
Leibniz, G.W. (1973), *The Monadology* in *Philosophical Writings*,
    ed. G.H.R. Parkinson, London: J.M. Dent   64
Lewis, H.D. (1965), *Philosophy of Religion*, London: English
    Universities Press   9
Middleton, J. R. and Walsh, B. J. (1995), *Truth is Stranger than
    it used to be: Biblical Faith in a Postmodern Age*,
    London: SPC   35, 36
Monk, R. (1991), *Ludwig Wittgenstein: The Duty of Genius*,
    London: Vintage   51
Montaigne, M. de (1595), *The Complete Essays*, trans. by
    M.A. Screech, London: Penguin, 1991   79
Nagel, E. (1961), *The Structure of Science*, London: RKP   57
Nagel, T. (1986), *The View from Nowhere*, Oxford: OUP   55
Nagel, T. (1987), *What Does It All Mean?* Oxford: OUP   55

Page Nos

Najder, Z. (1975), *Values and Explanations*, Oxford: Clarendon
    Press,   82
Passmore, J. (1968), *A Hundred Years of Philosophy*, London:
    Penguin   17
Penrose, R. (1990), *The Emperor's New Mind*, London: Vintage   59
Penrose, R. (1995) *Shadows of the Mind*, London: Vintage   59
Plato, (1973), *Phaedrus*, London: Penguin   120
Popper, K. (1968), *The Logic of Scientific Discovery*, London:
    Hutchinson   36
Popper, K. (1972), *Objective Knowledge*, Oxford: OUP   113
Popper, K. (1976), *Unended Quest*, London: Fontana   113
Popper, K. (1977), *The Self and its Brain*, London: RKP   113
Raven, A. (1932),*Civilisation as Divine Superman*,
    London: Williams & Norgate   115
Reid, T. (1895), 'Essays on the Active Powers of Man',   67
Reid, T. (1895), Letter to Dr. Gregory, *Reid's Works*,
    ed. Sir W. Hamilton, Edinburgh,   53
Robinson, J.A.T. (1963), *Honest to God*, London: SCM Press   40
Rucker, R. (1997), *Infinity and the Mind: the Science and
    Philosophy of the Infinite*, London: Penguin   114, 115
Runes, D.D. (ed.), (1977), *Dictionary of Philosophy*,
    New Jersey: Littlefield, Adams   17
Russell, B. (1974), 'On the Notion of Cause', *Mysticism and
    Logic*, London: Unwin   67
Russell, B. (1975), 'Has Religion Made Useful Contributions to
    Civilisation?' *Why I am not a Christian*, London: Unwin   23
Ryle, G. (1968), *The Concept of Mind*, London: Penguin   50
Schopenhauer A. (1844), *The World as Will and Representation*
    New York: Dover Publications, 1969   51
Schopenhauer A. (1847), *The Fourfold Root of the Principle
    of Sufficient Reason*, La Salle, Illinois, 1974   51
Schuon, F. (1959), *Gnosis: Divine Wisdom*, London: John Murray   25
Searle, J. (1983), *Intentionality: An Essay in the Philosophy of
    Mind*, Cambridge: CUP   59
Searle, J. (1996), *The Construction of Social Reality*, London:
    Penguin   64
Shaftesbury, Earl of (1964), *Characteristics*, ed. J.M. Robertson,
    New York: Bobbs-Merrill   23

Page Nos

Shaw, G.B. (1971), *Man and Superman*, London: Penguin   73
Siegel, H. (1988), *Educating Reason*, New York: Routledge   10
Spencer, H. (1945), *First Principles*, London: Watts & Co.   128
Sylvester-Bradley, P.C. (1971) 'An Evolutionary Model for the
    Origin of Life', *Understanding the Earth*, Artemis Press   101
Taylor, C. (1977), *Hegel*, Cambridge: CUP   58
Teilhard de Chardin, P. (1959), *The Phenomenon of Man*,
    London: Collins   13, 49
Teilhard de Chardin, P. (1959), *The Future of Man*, London:
    Collins   103
Teilhard de Chardin, P. (1972), *Letters to Two Friends*,
    London: Collins   104
Tipler, F. J. (1995) *The Physics of Immortality*, London:
    Macmillan   126
Turnbull, C. (1984), *The Mountain People*, London: Paladin   34
Veening, E.P. (1994), 'Metalogue as a Key-Concept in the
    Methods of Philosophical Counseling' - First International
    Conference on   Philosophical Counseling in Vancouver   114
Vernadsky, V. I. (1926), *The Biosphere*, London: Synergetic
    Press Inc., 1986   104
Wells, H.G. (1902), *The Discovery of the Future*, ed. by P.
    Parrinder, London: PNL Press, 1989   3, 128, 129
Williams, B. (1987), *Ethics and the Limits of Philosophy*,
    London: Fontana   9
Wittgenstein, L. (1958), *Philosophical Investigations*,
    Oxford: Blackwell, 1968   50, 84, 85
Wolpert, L. (1993), *The Unnatural Nature of Science*,
    London: Faber and Faber   12
von Wright, G.H.   (1962), 'Biographical Sketch' in
    Ludwig Wittgenstein: A Memoir, London: OUP   51
Wright, T.R. (1986), *The Religion of Humanity: The Impact of
    Comtean Positivism on Victorian Britain*, Cambridge:
    CUP   11

General Texts:

Biblical Texts: Genesis, ch. 12, verses 5-8   31
      Jeremiah, ch. 17, verses 5 and 7   31
      Matthew, ch. 4, verses 7-8   32
      I Corinthians, ch. 2, verses 10 - 16   58
Buddhist Scriptures, trans. E. Conze, London: Penguin, 1979   34
Encyclopaedia Britannica, Vol. 25   104
The Holy Qur'ân, trans. Abdullah Yusuf Ali, London: The Islamic
   Foundation, 1975   33
Oxford English Dictionary   3

Name Index

Subject Index